THE BOOK OF
RELIGIOUS HOLIDAYS AND CELEBRATIONS

Books by Marguerite Ickis

THE BOOK OF CHRISTMAS
THE BOOK OF FESTIVAL HOLIDAYS
THE BOOK OF PATRIOTIC HOLIDAYS
HANDICRAFTS AND HOBBIES FOR RECREATION AND RETIREMENT
STANDARD BOOK OF QUILT MAKING AND COLLECTING
THE BOOK OF RELIGIOUS HOLIDAYS AND CELEBRATIONS

The Book of Religious Holidays and Celebrations

Marguerite Ickis

With drawings by Richard E. Howard

DODD, MEAD & COMPANY   NEW YORK

Linc

TO MY GOOD FRIENDS
Olive and Gilbert Kilcarr
who contributed much to this book

PREFACE

Religious holidays are joyous occasions. They are one of the forces that unite churches and give continuity to religious thought and purpose. Since all religions are deeply rooted in the past, the festivals naturally include many century-old customs and rituals which people in America still use. This book is full of pageants, ceremonies, rituals, drama, folk dances, and music, and it has been one of our purposes to help members of different faiths to understand them.

Religious holidays are like a gift of language; they give a religious interpretation without reference to specific doctrine identified with the great historical religions in America. In all holidays, we have emphasized the "pageantry" of the festival because it comes nearer the heart of the religious conviction of the individual than most people can get through theological tomes and commentaries.

There are many movable religious holidays that fall on different days in different years. All Jewish holidays are movable feasts; and Easter, the greatest Christian festival, falls on the first Sunday after the full moon crosses the spring equinox. For this reason most churches begin their calendar year in the fall; the Jews begin their religious year in Hebrew month of Tishra, which is September. The liturgical celebrations in the Catholic Church form an organic unit which consists of three festivals or seasons: Christmas (with Advent), Easter (with Lent), Pentecost (with rest of the year).

The Protestant Church divides its calendar according to the four seasons—winter, spring, summer, and fall. The first of September marks the beginning of the church year.

vii

Obviously not every religious holiday can be included in this book, but many of the dramatic forms and ideas can be adapted to other festival days of the year. Since *The Book of Religious Holidays* is one of a series of holiday books by the author, only the four Christian deity festivals—Christmas, Easter, Pentecost, and Holy Trinity—are included. Other religious celebrations, such as All Saints' Day and Thanksgiving, are described in detail in *The Book of Festival Holidays*. Civic holidays that are included in most church calendars may be found in *The Book of Patriotic Holidays*. Since Protestants celebrate fewer religious holidays than do Catholics or Jews, the author has included a number of special days that are observed by Protestant churches throughout the year.

CONTENTS

PREFACE   vii

1. JEWISH HOLY DAYS   3

Go Down Moses — Jewish Prayer for Peace — Sabbath — Purim —
Yom Kippur — Hanukkah, Festival of Lights — Hamishah Asar
Bishvat — Pilgrim Festivals — Passover — The Haggadah — The
Seder Symbols — The Four Questions — The Seder Service — Shav-
not, A Festival of the First Fruits — Sukkot — The Mezuzah

2. FESTIVAL CYCLES   35

The Cross — The Maltese Cross — God's Christmas Promise

3. CHRISTMAS CYCLE   40

Advent — Advent Wreath — Star of Seven — St. Nicholas Day —
A Flowering Branch

The First Christmas — Christmas, A Holy Day — Protestant Ser-
vices — The Catholic Service — The Christmas Tree — Legend of
St. Boniface — Story of St. Winfred — The Lighted Christmas Tree
— Christmas Tree in America — Christmas Candles — Candle in the
Window — "White Lighting" — "Carols by Candlelight" — The Giving
of Gifts — Santa Claus — Christmas for God's Creatures — Bringing
in the Yule Log — Blessings — The Christmas Crib — Children's
Prayer — Nativity Scenes — Office of the Shepherds — Christmas in
American Cities — A Modern Bethlehem — The Birds' Christmas
Tree — Christmas in Hawaii — A Christmas Gift to the People —
"Christmas Carols Are for Everyone" — Seattle's Christmas Ship —
An International Christmas — A Christmas Candelabra — Christmas
Cheer Week — Largest Nativity Scene — Largest Living Christmas
Tree — Fort Myers' Singing Christmas Tree — Charlotte Singers'
Christmas Tree — Christmas Legends — The Christmas Angel —
Legend of the Pine Tree — Robin Red Breast — Legends of Christ-
mas Flowers — Christmas Carols — The Waits — A Christmas Love
Feast — Moravian Cookies

New Year's — The Old Year — Forgive Me for the New Year —
Visiting Day — The Gay New Year — Ringing Out of the Old Year
— New Year's in Other Lands — Japan — Chinese New Year —
Diwali, Indian New Year — Africa — Syria and Lebanon — Norooz,
New Year's Day in Iran — Why People in Taiwan Say "Kiong-hee"
at New Year's
January 6, Epiphany or Twelfth Night — Adoration of the Magi
— The Star Song — Feasts of the Epiphany — Celebration by Greek
Orthodox Church — Sanctification of the Waters — Feast of Lights
— Plundering the Christmas Tree — King of the Bean — The Twelfth
Cake — Mary Queen of Scots Party

4. EASTER CYCLE   110
Pre-Lenten Celebration — World Day of Prayer — Brotherhood
Sunday — Taking Leave of Alleluia — Lent — Ash Wednesday —
Mothering Sunday — Laetare Sunday — Holy Week — Palm Sunday —
Domingo de Ra (Palm Sunday in the Philippines) — *Tenebrae* —
Holy Thursday — Good Friday — Holy Saturday
The Easter Vigil — Blessing of the Easter Fire — The Paschal
Candle — Easter Mass — Greek Church Easter Vigil — Protestant
Celebration — Joyous Easter — Pageantry of Easter — Sunrise Ser-
vices — God's Acre — Easter Parades — The Easter Rabbit — Egg
Rolling — Lenten Foods — Symbols of Easter Day

5. PENTECOST CYCLE   138
Pentecost — Holy Trinity — Other Religious Celebrations — Corpus
Christi — Mother's Day — Children's Day — Rally Day

6. RELIGIOUS DRAMA   145
Theater in the Round — Masked Play or Masked Pantomime —
Asian Drama Form — Mime — Mystery Plays — *The Shepherds*

7. BIBLICAL GARDENS   151
Herbs from the Holy Land — A "Mary" Garden — Peace Gardens

8. NOTES   156
The Four Evangelists — Star Symbols — The Heavenly Host —
Ecclesiastical Colors

SUGGESTED SOURCES FOR ADDITIONAL HOLIDAY
MATERIAL   161

THE BOOK OF
RELIGIOUS HOLIDAYS AND CELEBRATIONS

Go Down Moses

(Spiritual)

When Israel was in Egypt's land,
Let my people go!
Oppress'd so hard they could not stand,
Let my people go!

Go down Moses, way down in Egypt's land;
Tell old Pharaoh, "Let my people go!"

"Thus saith the Lord," bold Moses said,
"Let my people go!
If not, I'll smite your first-born dead,
Let my people go!"

Go down Moses, way down in Egypt's land;
Tell old Pharaoh, "Let my people go!"

The Lord told Moses what to do,
Let my people go!
To lead the children of Israel thro',
Let my people go!

Go down Moses, way down in Egypt's land;
Tell old Pharaoh, "Let my people go!"
When they had reached the other shore,
Let my people go!
They sang a song of triumph o'er,
Let my people go!

Go down Moses, way down in Egypt's land;
Tell old Pharaoh, "Let my people go!"

1. JEWISH HOLY DAYS

Being an extraterritorial group, Jewry always needed strong inner ties. The holy days have been such ties. They have kept the past alive and fostered basic teachings of their faith. Each has its own distinctive philosophy, its own history, and its special ceremonial.

Two characteristics mark the whole cycle of Jewish holidays:

1. They are religious in character. The Bible orders them as "Feasts of the Lord." There are no secular holidays in Judaism; what might have remained secular events in history became religious institutions.

2. All Jewish holidays revolve around the people of Israel, or are in some way related to Israel. They commemorate events in the experience of a whole people rather than one personality.

3

Passover commemorates the time when all Israel found release from servitude.

Sabbath, the New Year, and the Day of Atonement are days of general religious observance rather than memorials of any particular event in the life of Israel.

Shavuot memorializes the giving of Law to Israel.

Sukkoth is a reminder of the harvest the Judean masses gathered.

Purim recalls the time when all the Jews were delivered from disaster.

Hanukkah extolls the valor of the Maccabees and restoration and rededication of Jewry's central shrine.

All Jewish holidays begin with the sunset of the preceding day, for the day according to the Hebrew calendar begins with the evening: "And there was evening, and there was morning the first day," reads the account of Creation in Genesis.

JEWISH PRAYER FOR PEACE

Reader

Grant us peace, Thy most precious gift, O Thou eternal source of peace, and enable Israel to be its messenger unto the peoples of the earth. Bless our country that it may ever be a stronghold of peace, and its advocate in the council of nations. May contentment reign within its borders, health and happiness within its homes. Strengthen the bonds of friendship and fellowship among the inhabitants of all lands. Plant virtue in every soul, and may the love of Thy name hallow every home and every heart. Praised be Thou, O Lord, Giver of peace. Amen.

The Jewish Education Committee Press, 426 West 58th Street, New York, New York, has many helpful publications. Notable are three books by Dvora Lapson on folk dancing and a number of songbooks for children. They have kindly given permission to reproduce three of Dvora Lapson's dances and four songs in *The New Jewish Songbook.* "What's Our Sukkah For" and "Who Will Sing Me One" are taken from *Songs We Sing.*

4

Slowly

May the words of my mouth and the me- di-ta-tions of my heart be ac- cept- a-ble in Thy sight, O Lord, my strength and my Re- deem- er. A- men.

SABBATH

Remember the Sabbath Day, to keep it holy. Six days you shall labor and do all your work; but the seventh day is a Sabbath to the Lord your God.

Of all the holidays and festivals, Sabbath is the only one mentioned in the Ten Commandments. So important is this weekly day of rest and spiritual renewal in the Jewish religion that it is honored in its departure, as well as its arrival, by a special ceremony. The Sabbath end ceremony is called *havadalah*, from the Hebrew word meaning "to distinguish," because God distinguished and set aside this day from other days of the week.

A rich growth of legend and literature surrounds the Sabbath. The Jew personified Sabbath as a lovely bride, a charming princess, a gracious queen; and on Friday he receives his Sabbath bride with hymns of welcome in the synagogue and in the home. On Friday night, we are told, the Jew is accompanied on his way

OPENING SONG: HINE MA TOV

How goodly it is and how pleasant for brethren to dwell together!

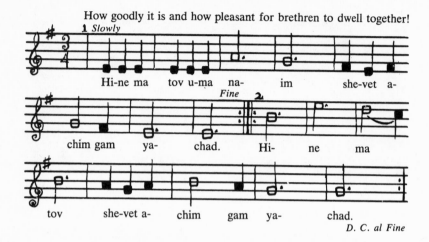

Hi-ne ma tov u-ma na- im she-vet a-

chim gam ya- chad. Hi- ne ma

tov she-vet a- chim gam ya- chad.

D. C. al Fine

LIGHTING THE SABBATH CANDLES

In the Jewish home, the table is set with bread and wine and the mother ushers in the Sabbath with the kindling of the candles. In the Reform Jewish synagogue, a woman is selected from the congregation each week.

Responsive Reading

Come, let us welcome the Sabbath. May its radiance illumine our hearts as we kindle these tapers.

Light is the symbol of the divine. The Lord is my light and my salvation.

Light is the symbol of the divine in man. The spirit of man is the light of the Lord.

Light is the symbol of the divine law. For the commandment is a lamp and the law is a light.

Light is the symbol of Israel's mission. I, the Lord, have set thee for a covenant of the people, for a light unto the nations.

Therefore, in the spirit of our ancient tradition that hallows and unites Israel in all lands and all ages, do we now kindle the Sabbath lights.

The candles are kindled

Blessed art Thou, O Lord our God, King of the universe, who hast sanctified us by Thy laws and commanded us to kindle the Sabbath light.

May the Lord bless us with Sabbath joy.

May the Lord bless us with Sabbath holiness.

May the Lord bless us with Sabbath peace.

Amen.

6

home from synagogue by two angels, one good and the other evil. When the Jew enters his home and the Sabbath lights are kindled and the home is radiant with joyous Sabbath atmosphere, the good angel blesses the home and says, "May this home always be an abode of happiness," and the wicked angel grudgingly answers, "Amen." But, if on coming home, he finds the Sabbath lights unlit and the house filled with gloom, the wicked angel curses the home and says, "May this home never know the joy of Sabbath." Then the good angel sighs and is forced to answer, "Amen."

The Sabbath service did not emerge from any specific period in Jewish history. It developed through the ages, and is celebrated in different ways, depending on the individual home and synagogue. Yet, within these variations, certain prayers and practices are common to all Jews.

Like all Jewish holidays, Sabbath begins the previous evening with sunset. No matter how poor a family, there is a clean white tablecloth, shining with the best plates and silverware. At the head of the table is a decanter of wine with ceremonial cups waiting beside it. Two loaves of freshly baked *hallah*—a braided white bread—rest beside the wine.

The home service begins when the mother lights the Sabbath candles. She praises God for His commandment of rest and peace and silently asks His blessing upon the home. This is followed by reading verses from Chapter 31 of the Book of Proverbs in honor of the good wife and mother:

A woman of valor, who can find? for her pride is above rubies. She looketh well to the ways of her household, and eateth not the bread of idleness.

Then the father raises his cup and recites the *Kiddush,* an ancient prayer sanctifying the Sabbath. After this, the father recites a blessing over the wine:

Blessed art Thou, O Lord, our God, Ruler of the universe, who brought forth bread from the earth.

Finally, over the bowed heads of his family, he asks God's blessing upon his children.

PRAISE TO THE LIVING GOD—YIGDAL

With dignity

Praise to the liv-ing God! All praised be His name. Who

was and is and is to be. For aye the same! The

one E-ter-nal God. Ere aught that now ap-pears. The

First the Last be- yond all thought His time- less years!

2 *He knoweth every thought,*
   Our secrets open lie,
   End as beginning dear
   To His all seeing eye.
   With perfect poise He binds,
   Accordant to the deed,
   To wrong the doom, to right the joy,
   In measured meed.

3 *Eternal life hath He*
   Implanted in the soul;
   His love shall be our strength
   And stay, while ages roll.
   Praise to the living God!
   All praised be His name,
   Who was, and is, and is to be,
   For aye the same!

PURIM

The story of Purim is told in the Book of Esther. It tells about a vain man named Haman who commanded that everyone who passed must bow down before him. One man refused—his name was Mordecai—and declared, "I bend the knee before God alone, the only living One in heaven above." Hearing this, Haman was so angered that he decided to kill not only Mordecai but *all* the Jews in the Persian Empire.

At the time, the Queen of Persia was Esther, a Jewish lady of great beauty and a cousin of Mordecai's. Now, as she learned from him what was about to befall her defenseless people, at a great risk to her own life she summoned up courage to ask the king for help. The only way he could help was to command that the Jews be allowed to arm and defend themselves. With God's help they did this successfully, and Haman was put to death on the gallows he had prepared for Mordecai.

On Purim eve in the synagogue, it is traditional to read the Book of Esther. At every mention of Haman's name, the children

MORDECAI'S PROCESSION

Verse: *J. K. Eisenstein*   *J. K. Eisenstein*

With martial spirit

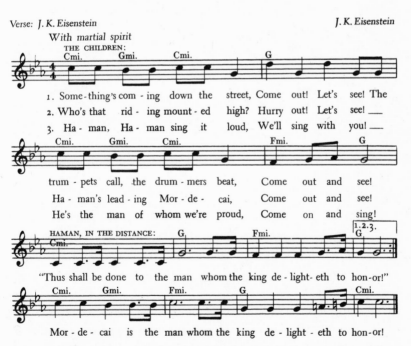

1. Some-thing's com-ing down the street, Come out! Let's see! The
2. Who's that rid-ing mount-ed high? Hurry out! Let's see! __
3. Ha-man, Ha-man sing it loud, We'll sing with you! __

trum-pets call, the drum-mers beat, Come out and see!
Ha-man's lead-ing Mor-de-cai, Come out and see!
He's the man of whom we're proud, Come on and sing!

HAMAN, IN THE DISTANCE:

"Thus shall be done to the man whom the king de-light-eth to hon-or!"

Mor-de-cai is the man whom the king de-light-eth to hon-or!

Purim is a time for *Purim Shpielers* (play actors). This song lends itself easily to dramatization. Select the required characters and they will improvise the called for action.

9

I LOVE THE DAY—PURIM

S.S. Grossman   S.E. Goldfarb

(1) I love the day of Pu-rim so! For then, to syn-a-gogue I go, And hear them read the sto-ry old Of Es-ther brave and Ha-man bold.

Chorus: O Pu-rim, O Pu-rim, O Pu-rim full of joy For ev-ery, for ev-ery Jew-ish girl and boy! (2)Have a par-ty, sing a song, Turn the gre-ger loud and long, Shlo-ach Ma-not give and take, Eat your Ho-men-tash-en cake! O Pu-rim, O Pu-rim, O Pu-rim, full of joy For ev-ery, for ev-ery Jew-ish girl and boy!

stomp, clap, and make all manner of noise with their noisemakers. In this fashion they symbolically blot out Haman's name and the memory of his evil.

In many ways Purim has the spirit of a social event; there are carnivals, parties, costume plays, dances, and last but not least, *hamantash* (a *homentash*), delicious three-cornered pastries.

YOM KIPPUR

Yom Kippur, or Day of Atonement, is a time for repentance, prayer, and charity. On this solemn and important day, almost all Jewish men and women refrain from eating and drinking.

The word "Atonement" explains the nature of the day. It is a day on which, above all, Jews seek forgiveness, not only from God but also from man. Judaism teaches that one cannot ask God's forgiveness unless he also asks others to forgive him any evil he might have done. The wrong must be righted whenever it is possible.

In Yom Kippur services, the part best known and the best loved by the Jewish young people is the famous *Kol Nidre* prayer which is recited on eve of the holiday. It is not so much the words of the prayer that are stirring, but the awesome and inspiring melody. This beautiful melody has become so much a part of the world's great religious music that singers and musicians of many faiths have made recordings of it.

HANUKKAH—FESTIVAL OF LIGHTS

On December nights, one can see through the windows of Jewish homes small flickering candles set in an eight-branched candelabra proclaiming a miracle of redemption performed long ago at that season. The candle lights may be pale compared with the blaze of jeweled Christmas trees, but the eye can discern their frail unvanquished flames shining forth in praise of God. Hanukkah is not as important in Judaism as Christmas is in Christianity. Its observance is not ordained in the Hebrew Scriptures, and although songs of praise and special scriptural portions are read in the synagogues, and a brief service accompanies the kindling of the candles, the eight days of the festival are ordinary working days.

The week of Hanukkah is a gay and happy one. But underneath its gaiety and fun the celebration has beauty and significance in the rededication of the Jewish people to the ideals of the Maccabees—religious freedom and political liberty under God.

The primary source for the history of Hanukkah is in the First and Second Books of the Maccabees, which were written shortly after the events they describe. According to the Scriptures, the Syrian king, Antiochus, prohibited the practice of the Jewish religion in Judea. Town by town the king's men carried out his new edicts. The temple was desecrated, swine flesh was offered, and

11

idols were set up. Scrolls of the Torah were burned. This attempt to annihilate a traditional religion as a punitive measure was, perhaps, the first religious persecution in history. To the Maccabees belongs the signal honor of having been the first to fight for religious freedom.

Near Jerusalem was a town called Modin. It was in the marketplace that Mattathias, a priest of the descendants of Joarib, saw the impious things that were going on in Judea and Jerusalem. The king's officers said to Mattathias, "You are a leading man, great and distinguished in this town; now be the first to come forward and carry out the king's command, and you and your sons will be counted among the friends of the king."

Then Mattathias uttered these words, "God forbid that we should abandon the Torah and the ordinances. We will not listen to the message of the king." As he ceased to utter these words, a Jew went up before the eyes of all of them to offer sacrifice to the idol as the king commanded, and Mattathias, his heart stirred, ran up and slaughtered him upon the altar.

Then Mattathias cried out in a loud voice in the town and said, "Let everybody that is zealous for the Torah and stands by the Covenant come out after me." And he and his seven sons fled to the mountains and left all they possessed in the town. When the time drew near for Mattathias to die he told his sons, "Remember the deeds of our forefathers and give your lives for the Covenant and the Torah."

Then his son Judah, who was called the Maccabee, and all his brothers rose in his stead. They sounded the trumpets and gave a great shout, and Judah said, "Prepare yourselves and be brave men and be ready to fight these heathens who are gathered together against us, for it is better for us to die in battle than to witness the ruin of our nation and our sanctuary." When the men sounded the trumpets and attacked, the heathen broke and fled into the plain, and all the hindmost fell by the sword.

Then Judah and his brothers said, "Now that our enemies are crushed, let us go up to purify the sanctuary and rededicate it." They found the temple desolated, the altar polluted, the doors burned, weeds growing in the court, and the priests' quarters torn down. The miracle of Hanukkah is embodied in a simple cruse of oil. When the people reentered the temple they found a single cruse of oil, sufficient for only one day, yet they kindled lights from it for eight days!

There is still another commandment for this Festival of Lights. The Jews are enjoined to have the candles shine through the doorway of the house, thus proclaiming the miracle to every passerby. Their light, then, shines not only within, but toward the outer world as well. Hanukkah lights, torches, candles, menorahs, try to dispel the mist and to banish the darkness roundabout. The Hanukkah candles are public illumination seen by all. The lights of Hanukkah have no traffic with conspiracies; they leave no place for ambushes, for clandestine plans to destroy and kill.

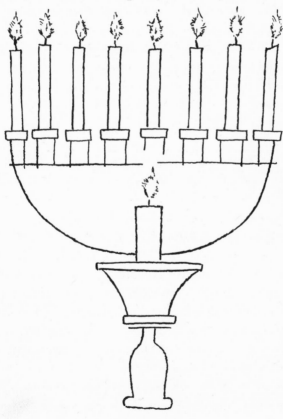

Liturgy, Observance, Customs. The Hanukkah Festival lasts eight days. The principal ceremony is the lighting of the Hanukkah lights each evening in the home or at the synagogue. On the first night, a single candle is lit, and an additional light is kindled on each successive night. The candles are arranged from right to left. There is a special place for an additional candle, the *"shamash,"* with which the other candles are lit.

The home is decorated with suitable Hanukkah motifs. The menorah traditionally is set in the window or in another prominent place, that all who pass by may see the Hanukkah lights and witness their meaning.

Menorah. This is the candelabra used to hold the eight Hanukkah candles. The middle candle is used as a taper for lighting the others. Each night during the eight-day festival, members of the family recite together their blessings and chant a prayer as one of the candles is being lighted. A single candle is lit the first night, two the second, and so on until the last day of the festival when all eight are burning. The eight candles represent these things: faith, freedom, courage, love, charity, integrity, knowledge, and peace.

Before the lights are kindled, the following blessings are said:

Praised are You, O Lord our God, King of the Universe, who sanctified us with Your commandments and commanded us to kindle the Hanukkah light.

Praised are You, O Lord our God, King of the Universe, who performed wondrous deeds for our fathers in ancient days at this season.

(*On the first night, add the following:*)

Praised are You, O Lord our God, King of the Universe, who kept us in life, sustained us, and enabled us to reach this season.

(*After lighting the Hanukkah candles, the assembled recite together:*)

These lights we kindle to recall the wondrous triumphs and the miraculous victories wrought through Your holy priests

14

for our forefathers in ancient times at this season. These lights are sacred through all the eight days of Hanukkah. We may not put them to ordinary use, but are to look upon them and thus be reminded to thank and praise You for the wondrous miracle of our deliverance.

The following additional activities are part of the Hanukkah celebration:

1. A special delicacy, "latkes" (potato pancakes), is served during one or more meals of the eight-day celebration.

2. Children, and adults as well, exchange gifts. Often parents and grandparents distribute Hanukkah "gelt," coins, to the younger set.

3. Parties for children, family, and friends are arranged.

4. Religious schools generally present special programs, parties, and assemblies for children, parents, and the general community.

5. Hanukkah games and dances, musical concerts, and dramatic presentations are popular. The most popular Hanukkah game is the "dreidel," a top with four sides, on each of which is a Hebrew letter.

6. Large menorahs are often placed in front of synagogues and temples during the Hanukkah festival. In the state of Israel, such menorahs adorn most important public buildings.

7. At synagogue services, the liturgy contains a number of additional prayers, including the following:

AL HANI'SIM

We thank you for the miracles, the heroism, the triumphs, through which You saved our fathers in ancient days at this season.
In the days of Mattathias, the Hasmonean, son of Yohanan the renowned priest, in his days and in the days of his son, a cruel power rose against Israel, demanding the abandonment of Your Torah and the violation of Your commandments.
You, in great mercy, stood by Your people in time of trouble. You defended them, vindicated them, and avenged their wrongs.
You delivered the strong into the hands of the weak, the many

15

MY DREDL

Verse: S. S. Grossman

S. E. Goldfarb

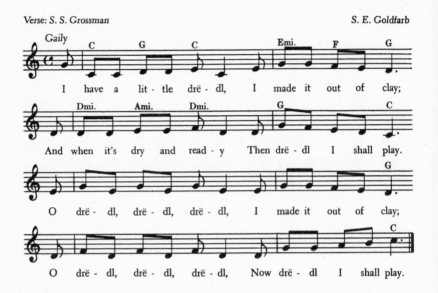

I have a lit-tle drë-dl, I made it out of clay;

And when it's dry and read-y Then drë-dl I shall play.

O drë-dl, drë-dl, drë-dl, I made it out of clay;

O drë-dl, drë-dl, drë-dl, Now drë-dl I shall play.

It has a lovely body,
　With leg so short and thin;
And when it is all tired,
　It drops and then I win.

My drëdl is always playful,
　It loves to dance and spin;
A happy game of drëdl,
　Come play, now let's begin.

　　O drëdl, drëdl, drëdl,
　　　With leg so short and thin;
　　O drëdl, drëdl, drëdl,
　　　It drops and then I win.

　　O drëdl, drëdl, drëdl,
　　　It loves to dance and spin;
　　O drëdl, drëdl, drëdl,
　　　Come play, now let's begin.

into the hands of the few, the corrupt into the hands of the pure in heart, the guilty into the hands of the innocent. You delivered the arrogant into the hands of those who were faithful to Your Torah. Because You wrought great victories and miraculous deliverance for Your people Israel to this very day, You revealed Your glory and Your holiness to all the world.

Then Your children came into Your shrine, cleansed Your Temple, purified Your sanctuary, and kindled lights in Your sacred courts. They set aside these eight days as a season for giving thanks and reciting praises to You.

16

HANUKKAH O HANUKKAH

Joyously

Folk Music

Circle Dance

Dance by Sara Levi

This charming little dance is suitable for kindergarten and first and second grade children. PART II may describe a dreidel turning. PART IV may interpret the turning on and off of lights. There is another dance to the same melody in the book, "Jewish Dances the Year Round" by Dvora Lapson.

FORMATION: Single circle, hands joined and down.

PART I. Facing clockwise, take 16 steps in line of direction.

17

PART II. Releasing hands, each one makes right turn in place (like a dreidel) pivoting with 8 pivot steps and 8 claps. (There are 2 complete turns to fill the music.)

PART III.

Phrase 1. Facing center of circle and joining hands, take 3 steps toward the center, gradually lifting hands forward and up, accentuating the 3rd step with a stamp of the foot.
Then hold 1 count.

Phrase 2. Lowering hands gradually take 3 steps backwards, accentuating 3rd step with a stamp of the foot.
Then hold 1 count.

Repeat movement of PART III Phrases 1 and 2.

PART IV.

Phrase 1. Releasing hands and raising right hand overhead, make a right turn in place with 8 pivot steps, accentuating each pivot step by extending fingers of hands slightly, then quickly bringing fingers together.

Phrase 2. On the repeat of the music of PART IV, do the same movements of PART IV Phrase 1, making a left turn in place with left hand held overhead.

Hanukkah, O Hanukkah

Oy Hanukkah, oy Hanukkah, a yontef a sheyner
A lustiger, a freylicher, nito noch azeiner
Ale nacht in dreydlach shpilen mir
Zudig heyse latkes est on a shir
Geshvinder, tzindt kinder, di dininke lichtelech on
Zogt, "al hanisim," loybt Got far di "nisim"
Un kumt gicher tantzen in Kon.

Hanukkah, O Hanukkah

O Hanukkah, O Hanukkah, a festival of joy,
A holiday, a jolly-day, for every girl and boy,
Spin the whirling trendles all week long,
Eat the sizzling "latkes," sing the happy songs!

18

Now light then, tonight then, the flickering candles in a row,
Retell the wondrous story, of God in all His glory,
And dance by the candles cheering glow.

TREE PLANTING (PROCESSIONAL)

Music by J. Admon

March tempo

(Group Dance)

Dance by Dvora Lapson

For centuries, the Jewish people all over the world have been identifying themselves with
the flora of their historic homeland, the Land of Israel, by celebrating a New Year of the
Trees (Arbor Day) on the fifteenth day of the month of Shevat. They partake of the fruits
(dates, figs, raisins, nuts and St. John's bread) which are native to that country while
pronouncing the appropriate blessings.

In modern times, with the resettlement of Jews on the land, this day is celebrated in Israel
by the planting of trees with special ceremonies.

Formation: All the children enter in single file. Each one holds in his right hand a spade
and in his left hand a sapling ready to be planted. In front of the stage stand
pots, one for each child, containing loose earth, in which the children will
plant the saplings at the climax of the ceremony.

PART I. In marching rhythm, to the beat of the music, the leader, at the head of the
group, leads them through the following formations:

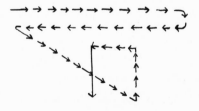

19

On the fifteenth day of the Hebrew month of Shvat, which falls in January or February by our modern calendar, many Jewish children observe the holiday of Hamishah Asar Bishvat—the New Year's of the trees.

In ancient Palestine, when trees were abundant, it was the custom of this day for a father to plant a cedar sapling for a male child born during the year, and a cypress for a female child. At their marriage the respective trees would be cut down and used as posts for the traditional wedding canopy.

Today, in Palestine, everyone recognizes the importance of replenishing the country's trees. More than just beautifying the country, they give shade and shelter; provide such fruit as pomegranates, almonds, dates, figs, oranges, lemons, and grapefruit. Also, they protect the people from hot, dry winds that sweep across the country.

Thus, in present-day Israel, Hamishah Asar Bishvat has become a day of planting new trees. The children are given the privilege of doing the planting and the ceremony is followed by cheerful parties. Jewish children in America celebrate by partaking of a variety of Palestinian fruit such as the ones mentioned above.

The children then turn off alternately right and left, walk to the rear and come down the center in double file, then later in quadruple file, after which they make their way to the rear of the stage again.

All are now standing in a horizontal line facing forward:

1 2 3 4 5 6 7 8 9 10 11 12

PART II.

Phrase 1. Odd numbers take 4 steps forward.

Phrase 2. Odd numbers do a complete right turn in place with 4 steps, until they face forward again.

Phrase 3. Even numbers take 4 steps forward, as odd numbers mark time in place.

Phrase 4. Even numbers do a complete right turn in place with 4 steps, until they face forward again. Odd and even numbers are now standing shoulder to shoulder.

Phrase 5. All come forward 4 steps.

Phrase 6. All make 3 digging movements with spade in the earth of the pot before them.

Phrase 7. All place the sapling in the earth with left hand and place spade beside the pot.

Phrase 8. Earth is pressed around the roots of the saplings.

Phrase 9. All clap hands 3 times.

PART III.

Phrases 1 and 2. Each one takes 4 polka steps around his own sapling, hands on hips, coming back to original place in line.

Phrases 3 - 9. The children at each end of the line take watering cans and pretend to sprinkle each sapling with water, dancing in and out among the pots. They all then form a line and dance around the room with skipping steps led by one of the children with the watering cans. The other forms the rear of the line. The leader may take them in and out among the pots and end the dance by skipping off the stage.

Tree Planting

Kach holchim hashotlim
Ron balev v'et bayad,
Min ha-ir umin hakfar,
Min ha-ir umin hakfar,

Lama vatem hashotlim
Nach bakarka u vats or
V'gumot saviv nachpor
Beharim uvamishor

Chorus: B'Tu Tu Tu Tu Bish'vat. *Chorus:* B'Tu Tu Tu Tu Bish'vat.

Ma y'he po hashotlim
Shtil yavo b'chol guma
Yaar ad yifro s tzilo
Al artsenu aguma

Chorus: Tu, Tu, Tu Bish'vat

21

Here Come Planters

Here come planters spade in hand,
See them swinging bravely by,
Little trees they bear on high.

On Chamisha Asar Bishvat,
On Tu-Tu-Tu-Tu-
On Tu Bishvat

What has brought you planters here?
We strike the rocky mountain side,
Drain the marshes far and wide.
On Chamisha Asar . . .

What will all your labors bring?
Trees will clothe the land so bare,
Giving shade and beauty rare.
On Chamisha Asar . . .

Words by Y. Sheinberg
Translation by Rose W. Golub

PILGRIM FESTIVALS

Passover, Shavuot, and Sukkot are the three great Jewish holidays described in the Bible as *pilgrimage festivals*. On each of these occasions was a harvest celebration, and the Jewish people were instructed to make a pilgrimage to Jerusalem to offer their thanksgiving:

Three times a year shalt all thy males appear before the Lord thy God in the place where He shall choose; on the Feast of the Unleavened Bread, on the Feast of Weeks, and on the Feast of Tabernacles; and they shall not appear before the Lord empty; every male shall give as he is able, according to the blessing of the Lord thy God which He has given thee.

From all parts of Judea these pilgrims journeyed to the central shrine on Mount Zion. The country roads and mountain passes were crowded with gay peasant throngs keeping the holiday. Every pilgrim carried his own offering on his own shoulder. These were olives, dates, figs, grapes, pomegranates, and sheaves of wheat. The rich gave no more, no less, and the king carried his own basket.

The leader, perhaps playing a flute, chanted pilgrim songs; the crowd joined in the chorus:

> I will lift mine eyes unto the mountains;
> From whence shall my help come?
> My help cometh from the Lord,
> Who made heaven and earth.

Thus the procession moved from town to town. Before each town the procession would halt. The leader invited the inhabitants to join: "Come let us go up to Zion to the house of the Lord our God." The natives joined in the throng and moved on. The landscape echoed with their song.

These three festivals have preserved their gay and joyous spirit to this day. The agricultural theme is in all celebrations, but in the course of time, all three festivals acquired historic significance which overshadowed its importance, partly because the Jewish people were not living in Israel. Passover has always been celebrated as man's right to freedom from slavery; Shavuot, in addition to celebrating the offering of the first fruits, commemorates the giving of the Ten Commandments; and Sukkot recognizes man's reliance on the Almighty along with the thanksgiving for the harvest.

PASSOVER ("PESAH," IN HEBREW)

Of all the Jewish festivals, Passover is the most vivid and dramatic. No other celebration has developed as distinctive a home ritual, the Seder, with its special prayer test, the Haggadah. To find the beginning of the story of Passover, one must go back in history to the Book of Exodus, where it is told how the Jews were enslaved by Pharaoh and led to freedom by Moses.

When the Jewish people came to Egypt at the time of Joseph, they were welcomed. Then a Pharaoh arose who was hostile to them. He enslaved them, murdered their male babies, and made life impossible for them.

The Lord sent one plague after another upon the Egyptians until they reluctantly allowed the Hebrews to leave. Under the leadership of Moses, the Red Sea opened so the Hebrew slaves could escape the pursuing Egyptians and go to a new life in Israel.

So important is the emancipation story that the whole Passover ceremony is built around it. On Passover eve, the entire family gathers at the dinner table for the traditional Seder, which is both

24

a meal and a service of worship. The Seder attunes the partici-
pants to the meaning of the Egyptian bondage and renews the
joy in freedom and redemption which derives from the Exodus.
The great pilgrimage festival of later times, when thousands
streamed into Jerusalem to join in the paschal offerings, is also
recalled at the Seder service.

The Haggadah

The *Haggadah* is the book of worship used at the Seder service.
Haggadah means the *retelling* or the narration of the Exodus story.
It is a response to four passages in the Bible, which offer the following behest: "And you must tell your son on that day saying,
'This is done because of what the Eternal one did for me when I
left Egypt' . . . you shall therefore keep this ordinance in its due
season from year to year." Besides telling the story of Exodus, it
gives the order of ceremonies to be observed at the Seder and also
a running commentary of prayer, legend, hymn, and explanation.

The Seder Symbols

The traditional Seder table is made as attractive as possible,
with lighted festival candles, the finest linens and silver, and the
following Passover symbols:

The Seder plate is placed at the table near the leader of the
Seder. Arranged on it are—

A roasted shank bone, a reminder of the Paschal Lamb.

A roasted egg, a symbol of the festival sacrifice offered up in
the Jerusalem Temple.

Maror. The bitter herbs (horseradish) are a reminder of the
bitterness of the Egyptian slavery.

Haroset, a mixture of apple, nuts, cinnamon, and wine, which
represents the mortar without straw the Israelite slaves used in
Egypt.

Parsley. This is dipped into a dish of salt water before eating,
which is symbolic of the coming of spring and the perpetual renewal of life.

Three matzos, in commemoration of the unleavened bread

25

which the Jews baked in the desert when they fled from Egypt.

Four cups of wine. The drinking of wine by each participant at four points in the Seder symbolizes the fourfold promise of redemption in Exodus 6:6–7.

Cup of Elijah. This usually is a tall goblet which is placed in the center of the table. It is filled midway through the Seder. It is symbolic of hospitality, which is part of the mores of the Jewish people.

A cushioned armchair for the leader, or a pillow placed on his chair. This symbolizes the freedom enjoyed by the Israelites when they were redeemed from bondage. In ancient times only free men could enjoy the comforts of leisurely dining.

Afikomen or dessert. One of the three matzos is broken in half. The half that is put away to be eaten at the close of the meal is called the Afikomen. After it is distributed and eaten, no other food is taken. One of the customs connected with the Afikomen is a game of playing forfeits. The leader good-naturedly takes no note of the spiriting away of the hidden matzo by the children. They do not surrender the Afikomen until the leader redeems it with a gift or a promise of a gift.

The Four Questions

To sustain the interest of children in the Passover story and to make them understand the significance of the miraculous deliverance from Egyptian servitude, four relevant questions are asked by the youngest child present at the ceremony:

Why is this night different from all other nights? On all other nights, we eat either leavened or unleavened bread; why, on this night, only leavened bread?

On all other nights, we eat all kinds of herbs; why, on this night, bitter herbs especially?

On all other nights, we need not dip herbs at all; why, on this night, do we dip them twice?

On all other nights, we may sit at the table either erect or reclining; why, on this night, do we recline?

The Seder Service

1. THE KIDDUSH

The first cup is filled and the leader and celebrants
recite the following blessings:

Praised art Thou, O Eternal our God, Ruler of the universe,
Creator of the fruit of the vine. Praised art Thou, Who has chosen
us, exalted and sanctified us through Thy commandments. Out of
Thy love, Thou hast given us appointed seasons for rejoicing,
even this Festival of Unleavened Bread, the time of our freedom,
a sacred remembrance of the departure from Egypt. Praised art
Thou, O Eternal, Who sanctifies Israel and the festive seasons,
Who has preserved us, and sustained us, and brought us to this
season.

The celebrants drink the first cup of wine.

2. THE HANDS WASHED

Pitcher, basin and towels are brought round to each celebrant.

3. THE GREENS EATEN

The leader takes the parsley, lettuce or watercress from the Seder
Plate and distributes it to the celebrants.
They dip the greens in salt water and say in unison:

Praised by Thou, O Eternal our God, Ruler of the universe, Creator of the fruit of the earth.

The greens are then eaten.

4. THE AFIKOMEN

The leader breaks the middle matzo,
leaving one-half on the Seder Plate.
The other half, the Afikomen, is hidden and will be eaten
at the end of the meal.

5. THE PASSION STORY RECITED

"THIS IS THE BREAD OF AFFLICTION"
The leader uncovers the matzo on the Seder Plate.

He lifts it up for all to see, and the company recites together:

This is the bread of affliction which our ancestors ate in the land of Egypt. Let all who are hungry enter and eat. Let all who are in want come and celebrate the Passover with us. This year we are here; next year in Jerusalem. Yesterday we were slaves, today we are free men.

The matzo is set down. Wine is poured for the second cup.

SHAVUOT (FEAST OF WEEKS)
A FESTIVAL OF THE FIRST FRUITS

Shavuot, arriving just as spring is about to turn into summer, is a holiday of threefold joy and pleasure. It was first celebrated in Biblical days as the conclusion of grain harvest when the Hebrews brought their first fruits to Mount Zion. In later years, Shavuot was identified as the holiday commemorating the revelation of the Ten Commandments to Moses at Sinai.

It was customary to bring to the temple at Jerusalem as an offering to God two loaves of bread baked from the new wheat crop. From Shavuot to Sukkot, an unending parade of Jewish families would come to the temple with their harvest in thanksgiving. Today, in the synagogue, it is customary to read from the Book of Ruth, which tells, in part, how the Hebrew farmer was instructed by God to leave a corner of his field and the gleanings for the poor.

SHIBBOLET BASSADEH

Moderately

Music by M. Shelem

Circle Dance

Dance by Sara Levi

This charming little dance is suitable for kindergarten and first and second grade children. The movements of PART I may interpret either waving corn or planting of seeds. PART II may describe watering the earth; PART III cutting the grain. There is another dance by Lea Bergstein to the same melody which appears in the book, "Dances of the Jewish People" by Dvora Lapson.

FORMATION:	Single circle, each one facing counterclockwise, left hand on left hip with palm up, palm of right hand placed on palm of left hand.
PART I.	
Phrase 1.	Lift right hand from the left side, describing an arc overhead to the right side, while taking 1 step forward with right foot, bending knee slightly.
Phrase 2.	Return right hand to the palm of left hand, describing an arc, while closing left foot to right foot.
	PART I Phrases 1 and 2 is done 8 times.
PART II.	Making a ½ turn left to face clockwise and joining hands in circle, all take 16 steps in line of direction.
PART III.	Release hands and face center.
Phrase 1.	Take 1 step towards center, bending knees, crossing hands low, then uncrossing them, with staccato movements.

As the holiday became recognized as the time of giving, it attained a more spiritual nature. Thus on Shavuot eve many people observe the holiday by reading the Bible and studying other religious books.

OR HAVATZALOT	LIGHT OF LILY
Or havatzalot, zemer shoshanim	Light of lily, rhyme of rose
Basharon ala rei-ah adanim	In the Sharon fragrance grows
Havatzelet lach, li hashoshanim	Yours the lily, mine the rose
Basharon ala rei-ah adanim	In the Sharon fragrance grows
By Sara Levi	Translated by Leo Haber

One of the prettiest Shavuot customs is the decoration of the house with plants and flowers. The greens recall the green mountains of Sinai, where the Commandments were given, as well as the fruits of the ancient harvest festival.

SUKKOT (TABERNACLES)

Like Passover and Shavuot, Sukkot is of agricultural origin, decreed in the Bible as a harvest festival. Sukkah (sometimes spelled "suka") means "hut," the temporary abode of those who lived in the fields during the harvest season. Observant Jews to this day build a sukkah, outdoors if possible or in the synagogue proper. This is made of scraps from field and forest and decorated with produce from the harvest. Much art and poetry have been inspired by the family gatherings in colorful sukkahs. Every Jew is enjoined to visit the sukkah with his loved ones and friends and have at least one meal in it.

Rabbinic laws specify the sukkah's construction. It must symbolize the brevity and insecurity of human life. It must not be built of solid masonry; the roof must allow the stars to be seen and the rain to come through, reminding man of God beyond.

In time the festival acquired a historical significance and came to symbolize the tents in which the Israelites dwelt in the wilderness on their way to the Promised Land. This is part of the historic tendency in Judaism to emphasize memory of Egyptian

30

LAMA SUKA ZU? WHAT'S OUR SUKA FOR?

Eng. verse: F. Minkoff

Slowly, with feeling

Folk song

CHILD: La - ma su - ka zu, a - ba tov she - li?
CHILD: Lit - tle lea - fy house, with an earth - en floor,

La - ma su - ka zu, a - ba tov she - li? FATHER: Lë -
Tell me fa - ther do, What's this Su - ka for?

shëv ba - su - ka, ya - ki - ri, lë - shëv ba - su - ka, ha - vi - vi, Lë -
FATHER: For our pleas - ure, lit - tle son, ___ when the har - vest time is done. ___

shëv ba - su - ka, ye - led hën, ___ ye - led hën she - li. Lë -
Here we of - fer thank - ful prayers for na - ture's good - ly store.

shëv ba - su - ka, ye - led hën, ___ ye - led hën she - li.
Here we of - fer thank - ful prayers for na - ture's good - ly store.

CHILD:

Suka made of boughs
Open to the sky!
Built anew each fall—
Father, tell me why.

FATHER:

To remind us, little son,
To remind us, little one,
That our fathers tilled the soil
In ancient days gone by.

CHILD:

Here's a little box
Wrapped about and tied.
Tell me father, please,
What can be inside?

FATHER:

It's an "esrog," little one,
Bright and yellow as the sun,
Sent from far-off Israel,
The fruit of harvest-tide.

servitude, but Sukkot retains more of the agricultural than historic significance, with all the color of joy and harvest.

Beside the sukkah, the traditional symbols of the holiday are the *lulav* (a palm branch), the citron, myrtles, and willows. Pray-

31

ers for rain are a part of the Sukkoth liturgy. A day called Simchat Torah (the Rejoicing of the Law) has been added to this festival. It has become a festival dedicated to the reading of the Law, and the Scroll of Law is completed and begun again on this day.

THE MEZUZAH

Attached to the right-hand doorpost of the synagogue entrance is a most familiar Jewish symbol—the *mezuzah*. The mezuzah is also placed at the entrance of Jewish homes. It is a fragment of rolled parchment in a small case or chamber. The parchment includes the following Biblical verses in Hebrew:

Hear, O Israel, the Lord our God, the Lord is One.
And thou shalt love the Lord thy God with all thy heart,
And with all thy soul, and with all thy might.
And these words, which I command thee this day, shall be upon
  thy heart.
And thou shalt teach them diligently unto thy children, and shall
  talk of them when thou sittest in thy house, and when thou
  walkest by the way, and when thou liest down, and when thou
  riseth up.
And thou shalt bind them for a sign upon thy hand, and they shall
  be for frontlets between thine eyes.

32

EHAD MI YODEA? WHO WILL SING ME ONE?

Hagada
Eng. verse: F. Minkoff

Israeli

E - had mi yo - dë - a? E - had a -
Sing me one, Oh what can one be? I'll sing one, now

ni yo - dë - a: E - had E - lo - hë - nu, E -
lis - ten care - ful - ly: One is the Lord of hosts, The

lo - hë - nu, E - lo - hë - nu, E - lo - hë - nu, E - lo - hë - nu, E -
King of kings, the Ho-ly One, The Ho-ly One, blessed be He, The

lo - hë - nu, she - ba - sha - ma - yim
Lord our God is One, The Lord is One, who

u - va - a - rets, she - ba - sha - ma - yim u - va - a - rets.
reign- eth on high, He made the world to spin with- in the sky.

And thou shalt write them upon the doorposts of thy house and
upon thy gates (Deut. 6:4–9)

Sing me two, Oh what can two be?
I'll sing two, now listen carefully:
*Two tablets of the Law,
One is the Lord of hosts,
The King of kings, the Holy One,
The Holy One, blessed be He,
The Lord our God is One,
The Lord is One, who reigneth on high,
He made the world to spin within the sky.

33

Last verse: Sing me thirteen, Oh what can thirteen be?
I'll sing thirteen, now listen carefully:
* *Thirteen virtues of the Lord;*
* *Twelve tribes of Israel;*
* *Eleven stars in Joseph's dream;*
* *Ten stern Commandments;*
* *Nine are the Festivals;*
* *Eight lights for Hanuka;*
* *Seven days in every week;*
* *Six days, the earth was made;*
* *Five are the Torah's books;*
* *Four are the Matriarchs;*
* *Three are the Patriarchs;*
* *Two tablets of the Law;*
   One is the Lord of hosts,
   The King of kings, the Holy One,
   The Holy One, blessed be He,
   The Lord our God is One,
   The Lord is One, who reigneth on high,
   He made the world to spin within the sky.

*Sing these lines to the music of the second measure, second line, repeating the same music for each succeeding number. Then repeat the music again with the words "Ehad Elo-hë-nu" (One is the Lord of hosts) and continue with the rest of the song.

2. FESTIVAL CYCLES

The liturgies of all Christian churches revolve around the four festivals of the Deity—namely, Christmas, Easter, Pentecost, and Trinity Sunday. Of course, Christmas and Easter are the great days in both the Catholic and Protestant churches. Four other civic festivals adorn the yearly pattern of worship with their own color and significance. These include New Year's, Memorial Day, All Souls' Day, and Thanksgiving.

Catholic worship centers in the celebration of the Mass, but certain portions of the Mass can vary with the seasons. The liturgical celebrations from an organic unit which consists of three festival cycles or seasons. First is the Christmas cycle (with Advent and Epiphany), Easter (with Lent), and Pentecost (with the rest of the year). In between are various saints' days and other festivals, including those devoted to the memory and exaltation of Mary.

The liturgies in Protestant churches are divided into four seasons, and the first season on the church calendar begins in the fall. The autumn season commences with Rally Day on the first of September. Then follow All Saints' Day, World Peace Sunday (nearest November 11), Thanksgiving Day, Advent, and Christmas. The winter season begins with Epiphany and continues with

35

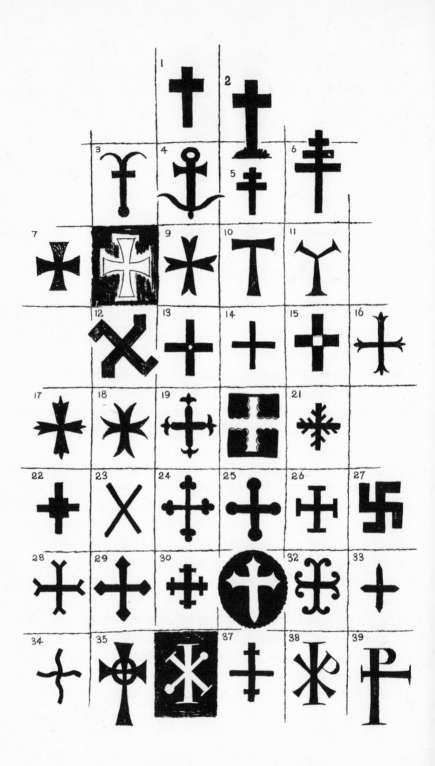

1. *Latin Cross*
2. *Calvary Cross*
3, 4. *Anchor Cross*
5. *Patriarchal Cross*
6. *Papal Cross*
7. *Cross Patee*
8. *Maltese Crossi*
9, 19. *Cross Moline*
10, 11, 12. *Tau Cross*
13, 28. *Fylfot (28. Crux Gammata or Swastika)*
14. *Cross Quarter Pierced*
15. *Greek Cross*
16. *Cross Quarterly Pierced*
17. *Cross Fleurie*
18. *Cross Patonce*
20. *Cross Fleurette*

21. *Cross Engrailed*
22. *Cross Ragulee*
23. *Cross Quaddate*
24. *Saltire (Crux Decussata)*
25. *Cross Botonnee*
26. *Cross Pommee*
27. *Cross Potent*
29. *Cross Fourchee*
30. *Cross Urdee*
31. *Cross Crosslet*
32. *Cross Fitchee*
33. *Cross Recercelee*
34. *Cross Pointed*
35. *Cross wavy*
36. *Cross of Iona*
37, 38, 39. *From the Catacombs*

Lent and Holy Week. Easter opens the spring season and includes Pentecost, Memorial Day, and Holy Trinity. The summer season varies greatly in Protestant churches, particularly in vacation areas. It is a time for special services and laying groundwork for the coming season.

All Christians are agreed on the glory of the Sunday worship. Civic legislation, too, has acknowledged Sunday as the general day of rest and worship in most countries of the civilized world. Sunday remains a day of deep spiritual joy and prayer for all people of the Christian world.

THE CROSS

The cross is a symbol of Christ's redemption of mankind and has become the most universal sign of Christianity. The cross in all variations has been used in art and heraldry for ages past, but the Latin Cross (Cross of Christ) is the most common. Other familiar crosses are the Cross of Lorraine, consisting of one short and one horizontal intersection toward the top, and the Celtic

Cross, including a circle in the upper portion, signifying the halo. The crosses shown on page 36 are explained by their names.

The Maltese Cross

The Maltese Cross is interesting as the emblem of service made famous by St. John's Hospitalers of Jerusalem during the Crusades, later called the Knights of Malta. It was an order of military monks, laymen, and knights whose office it was to relieve the poor, the stranger, and the sick. The eight points of the Maltese Cross represent eight Beatitudes, namely:

1. Spiritual joy
2. To live without malice
3. To weep over thy sins
4. To humble thyself to those who injure thee
5. To love justice
6. To be merciful
7. To be sincere and pure in heart
8. To suffer persecution

God's Christmas Promise

I will give the world tonight
My atomic star
And let its radiating glow
Fall on men afar.

I will burn within their hearts
An iridescent gleam,
And touch the spirit of the man
With its magic beam.

I will let this awe-ful fire
Destroy the world's long night,
Then sear the plagues of fear and hate
And flood their paths with light.

I will plant a desert spring,
A rose will grace the earth
And spread its fragrance everywhere
With peace and joy and mirth.

I will let an angel sing
What prophets used to shout.
While shepherds listen, see and tell
Wise Men will find it out.

I will give the world tonight
A love to set men free;
The strength for humankind's rebirth,
Living power to be.

Harold A. Schulz

3. CHRISTMAS CYCLE

Make ready for the way of the Lord.
(Matthew 3:3)

The sacred season called Advent (Coming) became widely observed in the ninth century and still is in Christian homes and churches. It begins on the Sunday nearest the feast of St. Andrew (November 30) and embraces the following four weeks, including Christmas Eve. While no special feast is prescribed, prayers and liturgical services stress preparation for the Lord's Nativity.

Advent traditions vary from place to place, but always the four-week period is looked upon as a happy time as people prepare for the greatest Christian festival of the year. Many beautiful customs are practiced in the home as well as in the church. Daily, at a certain time (usually in the evening), the whole family gather for a religious exercise and a moment of peace and contemplation. These ceremonies leave lasting impressions on the minds of children, remembering their love for the "day upon which a Savior was born to mankind."

Unfortunately in America, the Advent season has never been stressed as an integral part of the Christmas festival. For this reason, we are describing some of the age-old customs that parents might adopt as a reminder to their children that all the joys and pleasures of Christmas originate from the birth of the Holy Child.

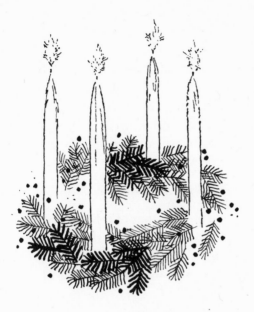

Advent Wreath

The Advent Wreath, an old Christian custom originating with the Lutherans in Germany, is being used in many American homes today. It is simply a circle of greenery around which four candles, one for each week of Advent, are equally spaced. They are usually lavender in color, symbolizing the penitence of the season. Sometimes one of the four candles is pink to signify the joy of Gaudete Sunday (third Sunday of Advent); or on Christmas Eve, the wreath may be made a part of the holiday decorations by replacing all four candles with red ones.

Make the wreath the center of attraction in the home—in the dining room, the children's room, or a large hallway. Some families prefer to suspend it from the ceiling or place it in front of the family shrine. One candle is lighted the first Sunday in Advent and an additional one each week thereafter, until on Christmas

41

Eve the wreath is a glowing testament of the nearness of the Savior. Each Sunday, upon lighting the candle, the family join to say a short prayer or read a verse from the Scripture. Often friends are invited to join the family circle to take part in the exercise and sing Christmas carols.

Star of Seven

Many German households have a "Star of Seven," which is a seven-branch candlestick. The candles are lighted on each Sunday in Advent—one on the first, two on the second, three on the third, and so on. Members of the family or groups of friends sit about the lighted tapers singing seasonal carols and preparing handmade gifts for Christmas.

St. Nicholas Day (December 6)

The role of St. Nicholas is that of a heavenly messenger coming at the beginning of Advent. It is on this feast day that the children's Christmas festival really begins. He is represented as a tall, venerable, kind-faced man, wearing the cape of a bishop with the miter headdress. With him one finds the dark-skinned companion known as Black Peter, who always carried a bunch of switches. He promises sweets to those who are good and threatens punishment to boys and girls who are bad unless they mend their naughty ways.

St. Nicholas rides a white horse followed by a cart laden with parcels to be left at different houses. Before they go to sleep, children stuff their shoes with hay and place them on the window sill so the horse will have something to eat during the journey. Of course, St. Nicholas always replaces the hay with candy and small gifts while Black Peter distributes switches to parents of children who are bad.

A Flowering Branch

It is customary in parts of Europe to break a branch off a cherry tree on the first Sunday in Advent and place it in a bowl of water. If it is kept in the kitchen or a place with warm air, it will burst into blossom on the last Sunday and make a festive decoration.

Sometimes children make tiny flowers out of feathers dyed in various colors and tie them onto the branch at the very beginning.

THE FIRST CHRISTMAS

It was because Emperor Caesar Augustus had ordered that a census be taken of all Roman subjects from the Rhine to the Jordan that Joseph had to return to the town of his birth to be counted. Taxes would be levied after the count. Even the lame and the blind had to make the journey.

Joseph, a descendant of David, returned with Mary to Bethlehem to comply with the Emperor's edict. He did not realize so many belonged to the House of David until he and his wife reached the inn. Some families were sleeping against the inn's wall; every field and every house were filled with people. The innkeeper's wife, feeling the chill of the night air and seeing that Mary was expecting a child, suggested that the man take his wife below to the stable where the animals were kept. At least they would have some privacy, however humble.

Before Jesus's birth, Joseph prayed, and when he looked up toward the east, he saw a strange thing. Over the Mountains of Moab three stars fused into one huge, bright star. At that moment the Infant gave His first cry. In this way the ancient prophecy was fulfilled: "Bethlehem Ephratah . . . out of thee shall He come forth unto me that is to be ruler of Israel."

The huge star was so bright that it filled the dark sky with light, awakening the shepherds who lived in carved apartments in the hills. In terror the herders listened to the words of an angel who floated over the valley. "Fear not, for, behold, I bring you good tidings of great joy, which shall be to all people. For unto you is born this day in the city of David a Savior, which is Christ the Lord. Ye shall find the Babe wrapped in swaddling clothes, lying in a manger."

So the shepherds, too overjoyed and excited to delegate someone to watch their flocks, followed the star to the town of Bethlehem. There they asked, where can the Messiah be found. Some wayfarers answered them rudely, but when they tried the inn the keeper remembered the man and wife lodging in the stable.

The shepherds went in haste and found Mary and Joseph, with the Babe lying in a manger. And when they saw, they understood what had been told them concerning the child. They knelt before the manger, murmuring prayers, piously clasping their hands before their chests. Then they left, praising God for the wondrous event.

Among the many men studying the blue-white star that night were the Magi—Gaspar, Melchior, and Balthazar. They were rich Persian philosophers and astrologers, the wise men of their country. They consulted ancient Greek, Persian, and Hebrew tracts to try to interpret the star's message. When they agreed it heralded the coming of a Savior in Israel, they left their tents to follow it before the star disappeared.

Later in Jerusalem, standing in Solomon's temple, they asked, "Where is the newborn King of the Jews whose star we saw in the east? We have come to offer homage to Him." The high priests detailed the Jewish belief about the coming of the Messiah, and the wise men decided to head to Bethlehem.

But when King Herod heard this, he was troubled and inquired of his scribes and priests where the Christ was to be born. And they said to him, "In Bethlehem of Judea, for thus it is written through the prophet,

'And thou Bethlehem, of the land of Judea,
    Art by no means least among the princes of Judah,
For from thee shall come forth a leader,
    Who shall rule my people Israel.' "

44

Then Herod summoned the Magi secretly and carefully ascertained from them the time when the star had appeared to them. Sending them to Bethlehem, he said, "Go and make careful inquiry concerning the child, and when you have found him bring me word, that I too may go and worship him."

The Magi continued on their camels to Bethlehem, questioning a few remaining pilgrims about the birth of a king in the area. Suddenly, the star that they had seen in the east went before them and stood over the place where the young child was. Upon entering the stable, they found the child with Mary, his mother, and falling to their knees worshiped him. After paying homage to the child, they opened up their treasures and offered gifts of gold, frankincense, and myrrh, then started on their homeward journey. Being warned in a dream not to return to Herod, they went back to their own country by another way.

The Innocents (Matthew 2:16–18). The mad King Herod feared that, if the news spread out over Judea that a new Messiah was born, the people would desert the temple and the king to worship the Infant. Seeing he had been tricked by the Magi, he was exceedingly angry and ordered the slaying of all the boys in Bethlehem and the neighborhood who were two years and under, according to the time that he had ascertained from the Magi. Then was fulfilled what was spoken through Jeremiah the prophet, saying:

> "A voice was heard in Rama,
> weeping and loud lamentation;
> Rachel weeping for her children,
> and she would not be comforted,
> because they are no more."

CHRISTMAS—A HOLY DAY

The hearts of all mankind are turned
Toward lovely Bethlehem;
For in the East the wondrous star that burned
In days of old
Still beckons them.

45

From earliest days of our nation, Americans have regarded Christmas as both a holy day and a holiday—a period of religious devotion and of general relaxation. Hymns and chants were the music of early Christian churches, but today we like to think a new kind of Christmas has emerged—one that is rich in carols and bells, candles and gifts, evergreens and firs, all to celebrate Christ's birth.

Christmas is a time not only of deep religious meaning in the church but of family happiness as well—"A Feast of Hearts," one man called it and to some it is "Happy Evening." Most families have their own traditional ways of celebrating Christmas. The tree stands each year in the appointed spot, a star or angel is placed on top, and the head of the family reads Charles Dickens's *Christmas Carol* and the story of the *First Christmas*. But underlying all the glitter and festivities, the spirit of good will to all and generosity to the poor is never forgotten.

The last century has seen Christmas emerge as a great American celebration of a kind not seen in any other part of the world. It includes ceremonials from many lands with improvisations and new aspects added with the years. However, although Christmas has a somewhat international flavor, it has a clear American accent. Indeed, it varies from North to South and from state to state, but still it is Christmas regardless of geography or climate.

Northerners like to think of a white Christmas with snowflakes glistening on the window sill and fields and gardens covered with snow. To the Southerner, it is a day of rich greenery and blooming flowers. In Pennsylvania the *putz*, or Nativity Scene, is displayed indoors either in front windows for the public to view or under the Christmas tree. In many parts of the South, "Christmas Gardens," depicting Christ's birth in a stable, are built outdoors in a natural setting of palm trees and large piles of rocks in the background to represent the mountains of Judea.

Among the isolated people of the ridges of mountains in Tennessee, Georgia, West Virginia, and Kentucky can be found a mountain Christmas with ancient, moving carols which have largely been lost to Americans. On long stretches in Texas, cowboys observe the Christmas holiday with square dancing and merrymaking. In other parts of the state the eloquent folk dramas of the Spanish Christmas are still alive.

One factor that makes Christmas the greatest Christian festival of the year is that the churches are in more fundamental agreement on the celebration than other holidays. Come December 1, Catholics and Lutherans, Methodists and Presbyterians, Episcopalians and other Protestants, look forward with eager longing to the coming of Christmas. It is heartening to see a whole community work together for a happy holiday and good will toward everyone.

Protestant Services

Christmas has always been a time beloved by Protestant Churches, and many customs adorn the festive season. The celebration begins with Advent and continues on to Epiphany, or Twelfth Night (January 6). Advent services are characterized by the spirit of expectancy. To emphasize the joy of the coming of the Savior on Christmas, the altar and pulpit appointments are changed to purple, the color of somber reflection. Sermons and scripture readings from the Bible set forth prophecies of the coming of Christ.

Every parish church celebrates Christmas at the Sunday morning service preceding the festive day itself. The program usually includes special Christmas music, the retelling of the Christmas story, and the pastor preaches a sermon which discusses the significance of Christ's birth in terms of the needs of the people in the church today. During the week other types of services take place—a "Service by Candlelight" on Christmas Eve, a cantata of sacred music, or a miscellaneous group of Christmas anthems by the choir. It is the custom in some churches to celebrate an "Old English Christmas" sometime during the holidays. Against a background of traditional greenery—ivy, holly, and mistletoe—the choir, dressed in Elizabethan costumes, sings early Christmas carols and songs from Shakespeare. Other church groups add to the program by taking part in short plays or pantomimes. If the

47

church has a fireplace, a Yule log is carried in and blessed by the pastor or head of the elders.

One special feature of the Christmas morning service has always been centered in the Sunday School. It gives parents and their children an opportunity to celebrate Christmas together in the church. At one time, elaborate programs, including recitations, skits, short plays, etc., were put on, but pressures of public schools and community centers leave little time for rehearsals. Raymond Alden's "Why the Chimes Rang" is still a favorite play for a children's program.

Two special Christmas programs, one celebrated particularly by Episcopalians and the other by Methodists, are widely presented in other Protestant Churches:

The Watch Night. For many years the Episcopalian Church has celebrated a midnight service of Holy Communion on Christmas Eve. The church and chancel are beautifully decorated with Christmas greens, with roses and poinsettias and other festival flowers. Often the entire church is illuminated with hundreds of flickering candles. Familiar hymns and carols are sung, and Holy Communion is celebrated to the accompaniment of some great choral setting such as Gounod's "St. Cecilia's Mass" or Handel's "Messiah."

White Gifts for the King. This custom was first used by a Methodist Church in Painsville, Ohio, in 1904, and is still observed the world around. It is based upon an old legend which told about the white feast and gifts of love on the great King's birthday. The service of "White Gifts for the King" does not involve material gifts; rather, gifts of self are brought, of service and of substance. Individuals are encouraged to write on cards certain commitments which they would make as a gift to Christ the King. These commitments might be matters of character development and personality change. They might also be for different forms of personal service that would be rendered during the coming months. Group gifts in terms of money are often made. All these gifts are brought to the foot of a white cross in a white chancel at the end of a Christmas service developed around this theme.

The Catholic Service

A Catholic would feel a deep regret if he did not join his friends for the solemnities of the holy night. The church is decorated with garlands of green and beautiful flowers as at no other time of the year. Altars are shiny white and silver and dotted with red flames from dozens of small white candles. These surround a great central one that symbolizes Christ, the Light of the World. Priests dressed in white and gold, assisted by acolytes, carry lighted tapers and pots of incense.

In many churches a solemn service of "Vespers" is held directly before the Midnight Mass. During the service, bells ring out through the winter night to announce the coming of the Savior. In some American cities, chimes and carillons accompany or replace the bells in the churches, ringing out tunes of familiar carols, especially the one of joyous invitation, "O Come, All Ye Faithful."

The unveiling of the Crib just before Midnight Mass is dear to the hearts of all Catholics. The drama reinforces their love for the Savior, and the groundwork is laid for a joyous celebration of the Nativity, not only in the house of God but also in the homes of the people.

The Three Masses. From early times the Three Masses have lived on as the very heart of the Christmas festival. They signify the mystical drama of the coming of the Savior:

The Missa in Nocte (during the night) to signify the Eternal Birth of the Word of God in the Father.

49

The Missa in Aurora (at dawn) to signify the Birth of the Son of God in the flesh, or the Temporal Birth.

The Missa in Die (during the day) to signify the Birth of Christ in the hearts of the faithful, the Spiritual Birth.

Midnight has never been assigned as the official time for the first Mass; it is merely prescribed that it be said during the night. In some churches it is celebrated before dawn at four or five in the morning; and in early centuries, it was celebrated about three o'clock "when the cock crows." In America most churches celebrate the first Mass at midnight except in states that border on Mexico; there they hold to the tradition of an early Mass.

The Midnight Mass. It is the custom in most Catholic churches to celebrate the first Mass at midnight because it is generally believed that Christ was born at that hour. On the stroke of midnight, the organ opens the processional with thunderous chords, and voices of the choir ring over the nave and aisles. Now a voice rings out in a hymn such as:

> Midnight, O Christian, 'tis the hour so solemn,
> When God as man descended from heav'n . . .

In Naples when the Gloria is sung at Midnight Mass, thousands of stars light up the church from sparklers which the people hold in their hands.

Associated with Midnight Mass is the informal *réveillon*, a late meal that follows soon afterward in the home. It combines reunion and thanksgiving as well as refreshments. In some homes the figure of the Christ Child is solemnly placed in the Crib while the family gather around to sing Christmas carols. Sometimes a Yule log is lit, and the father conducts a ceremony to ask a blessing on the house.

The Christmas drama is terminated on Epiphany, or Twelfth Night, with the altering of the Crib. Another star is placed over it, and the three Magi take the place of the shepherds. They are usually depicted as kings mounted on camels. In their hands are the traditional gifts of gold, frankincense, and myrrh.

50

THE CHRISTMAS TREE

In modern America, the Christmas tree is looked upon as a symbol of joy and good will to others and is the most beloved feature of the holiday season. There are many legends, indeed, concerning the Christmas tree, among which are the following.

Legend of St. Boniface

An ancient legend tells how in the eighteenth century St. Boniface persuaded the Teutons to give up their cruel practice of sacrificing a child before a great oak tree during their midwinter festival. Instead, he said, "Cut down a big fir tree, take it home, and celebrate around it with your innocent children." He also told them that the fir was the wood of peace, from which their houses were built, and that it was a sign of immortality, because its leaves were ever green and its top branches pointed straight to the heavens.

Story of St. Winfred

St. Winfred, a missionary to the Scandinavians in the eighth century, had another interpretation of the meaning of the tree. As he hewed down a great oak tree, a young fir tree miraculously, sprung up in its place. St. Winfred then proclaimed the tree holy, saying it was a symbol of endless life because its leaves are ever green. "Take it up and carry it to the Chieftain's hall. You shall go no more into the shadows of the forest to keep your feasts with sacred rites of shame. You shall keep them at home with laughter and songs and rites of love, gathered around the green fir tree to rejoice in the birth night of the Savior."

The Lighted Christmas Tree

It is generally agreed that the first person to put candles on a Christmas tree was the sixteenth-century German theologian Martin Luther. The Lutheran Hour's Dr. Hoffmann relates that while walking home one night shortly before Christmas, Martin Luther felt a strong tie between the lovely forest he was in, the starry heavens above, and his love for God. At home he placed tapers on a little evergreen tree to recapture the scene for his children by showing them how beautiful the stars looked through the high branches of the fir forests as they winked in the sky.

The custom of decorating a Christmas tree spread through Germany and eventually through Europe. It was introduced in England in 1841 by Prince Albert, Queen Victoria's German husband. The Christmas tree came to America as a cherished companion of the German immigrants. The fact that the royalty of England had adopted it did much to make it fashionable in homes of Americans of English descent.

Christmas Tree in America

A young pastor by the name of Schwan, in Cleveland, Ohio, created a furor in 1851 by bringing a lighted Christmas tree into his church. The town's decent people would not tolerate such a pagan practice! After long and weary research he proved to his congregation that it was a custom known even in America. It was this young pastor who first gave the lighted Christmas tree its now traditional place beside the altar of many an American church.

So the Christmas tree was carried into the church as well as the home. In an endeavor to give new meaning to heathen customs, purely Christian symbols were gradually introduced as decoration—the angels, the anchor, the cross and the heart, the Star of the East, and the golden threads (tinsel), called Sametta, which represent the hair of the Christ Child. The lights represent Christ, the light of the world.

How did the American custom of decorating outdoor trees begin? Mr. W. S. Lewis, of the Rocky Mountain Electric League, tells this story. "Christmas Eve in 1918 a little boy lay sick in his Denver, Colorado, home watching his father decorate the family tree. 'Daddy,' he said, 'I wish you could put lights on that tree out there,' pointing feebly to a splendid spruce in the front yard. 'Why, son, I believe I can. We'll dye some bulbs, fix a cord so the snow won't cause a short, and run it out from the basement.'" Elaborate illuminations are now characteristics of Christmas decorations in America.

Every year Americans spend about fifty million dollars for Christmas trees plus a few million more for baubles. This can be labeled as "big business." Recently this honored symbol has become an unbelievable swaggering array of lights and balls which overshadow the meaning of yesteryears.

However, the tree is the most beloved popular feature of the Christmas season. Along with the glittering balls, one usually finds symbols relating to the Christ Child and other decorations that remind one of an old-fashioned Christmas. Underneath the sparkling tree there may be a crèche with its manger scene and on top a star of some kind signifying the birth of a Savior. Among the branches are usually hung tiny angels, candy canes, cornucopias, toy trumpets, and other colorful ornaments. These precious features give a flavor to the tree that children will carry with them in later years as one of their cherished memories.

CHRISTMAS CANDLES

Burning candles at Christmastide is a custom which goes back to the Roman Saturnalia. During that period tapers were exchanged as tokens of cheerfulness and good will. The Jewish Feast of the Dedication, which came near the time of the Saturnalia, employed the use of candles, and it is not unlikely that at the time of the birth of Jesus, thousands of candles were burning

53

brightly throughout Palestine. Further evidence of this is the fact that the Greek Catholic Church calls Christmas "the Feast of Lights."

Candle in the Window

The lovely ritual of placing a lighted candle in a window at Christmastime was brought to America by the Irish. It was the dearest wish of every Irish family that a priest would arrive to celebrate the divine sacrifice during Holy Night. On Christmas night, they left their doors unlocked and placed lighted candles in the windows so any priest who happened to be in the vicinity could be welcomed and guided to their home through the dark night.

Since Boston is often called the "home of the Irish," it is not surprising that the custom of placing a lighted candle in the window on Christmas Eve has long been celebrated. In 1910 an American lady living in the old Beacon Hill section, Mrs. Ralph Adams Cram, persuaded a few friends to light their windows with candles on Christmas night. They set in the windows figures or paintings of the Madonna. Then they joined Mrs. Cram in singing carols from house to house. The next year more friends were induced to participate, and the circle widened until there were enough to form "The Chestnut Street Christmas Association." Now the windows of each house in this section of Boston are decorated on Christmas Eve with old family heirlooms—the delicately carved Madonnas, the rich tapestries and silverware handed down from great-great-grandfathers. Automobiles are barred from the streets, and the populace go wandering through them singing carols and calling on friends.

"White Lighting"

In Williamsburg, Virginia, candles are placed in the windows of exhibition buildings to burn from 5:00 P.M. to 10:00 P.M. December 24 to January 1. A watchman is assigned to each building as insurance against fire, and a saucer of water is placed under each candle.

54

The holiday season opens with a "White Light" ceremony on December 20 when children carry candles from the Palace, down Duke of Gloucester Street, to the Williamsburg Inn. The procession is led by the night watchman at the head of the fife and drum corps. Symbolically, the children "carry the flames to their homes," for candles are lighted as they pass by each window along the way. This is the beginning of the "white lighting" that gives Williamsburg its unusual and hyperhospitable glow during the holidays. It has so grown that now more than two thousand candles are displayed, in virtually every home, shop, and public building in this historical area.

"Carols by Candlelight"

On Christmas Eve twenty-five years ago, Norman Banks, radio announcer for Melbourne's Station 2KZ in Australia, was hurrying homeward from the studio. Passing through a certain street, he heard a soft, quavering voice joining in the words of a carol sung over a radio.

Peering through the window, Mr. Banks saw a touching sight. There sat a little, white-haired old lady, adding her gentle notes to the radio singer. To complete the Christmas effect, she was holding a lighted candle.

Somehow that scene made a deep impression on the radio man. He was inspired by an idea. Why couldn't the folks of Melbourne come together on Christmas Eve, each person carrying a lighted candle, and all join in the singing of carols? So was born the world's biggest Christmas carol-singing festival! From the time it was first launched down to the present, it is estimated that over a million persons have assembled for these "Carols by Candle-light" programs in various cities all over the globe!

Mr. Banks hardly expected the enthusiasm and cooperation he got from the very start. Careful preparations for the event are made far in advance. In recent years it has required a staff of about two thousand persons to attend to all the details. Just candles and candle holders alone have really become big business. After fifteen years in Melbourne, Mr. Banks sought to expand the festival to other parts of the world.

Probably no mortal on record has ever been responsible for so much happy singing on Christmas Eve, with the exception of the person whose birthday it is. As Chairman of the Carols by Candlelight World Foundation, Mr. Banks is continually seeking new audiences. The movement spread to New Zealand where he set up "Carols by Candlelight" in Wellington. He was also the leading spirit in bringing the festival to South Africa in Johannesburg and to British Columbia to the north. Sometime, he hopes, "Carols by Candlelight" will be sung on Trafalgar Square in London.

THE GIVING OF GIFTS

It has been the practice of people through the ages to set aside certain periods of the year in which, through the giving of gifts, they may share the good things of life with each other, particularly with those less fortunate. In early Roman days it was common practice to make presents during Calends of January. At this time "men gave honied things that the year of the recipient might be

56

sweeter, lamps that it might be full of light, silver and gold that wealth might attend them."

In Christian countries Christmas became the season for giving gifts. There are many forms of presenting gifts. In Germany a "Christmas ship" comes laden with bundles for the children. England observes the day following Christmas as "Boxing Day," when boxes of food are delivered to the needy. An old Holland custom explains why we have "piggy banks." There the children are trained to save their pennies in a pig-shaped earthenware container. This container was not to be opened until Christmas and consequently was called the "feast pig."

It is a tradition in the American Navy for the crews of battleships, cruisers, and destroyers to give a party and present gifts to poor children in whatever port they happen to be. Started in 1915 by the crew of the battleship *New York*, the idea spread quickly and spontaneously. Enlisted men are in charge of the party and of decorating the ship. The list of guests is generally provided by some charitable institution, and each child receives a personal gift from a bluejacket.

SANTA CLAUS

Santa Claus of today is in part an American contribution to the Christmas festival. Originally St. Nicholas, a lean, pale eccentric, carrying a dark miter and staff of a bishop, was the bearer of gifts to children. It was the work of three men that gave St. Nicholas the personality of our red-cheeked, white bearded, "Jolly Old Santa Claus."

First, Washington Irving presented America with the picture of a laughing holiday figure, very different from the early one in dark, somber robe. Then, in 1822, Dr. Clement Moore, a teacher in a New York seminary, composed a holiday poem for his children: "Visit From St. Nicholas." Its opening line, "It was the night before Christmas and all over the house," was soon known the world over. Beside being the creator of the American legend of Santa Claus, Dr. Moore has become an integral part of a Christmas Eve ceremony in a part of New York City. The children of

the Chapel of the Intercession make a pilgrimage with lighted candles across the street to his grave.

In 1836 the widely known cartoonist, Thomas Nast, drew the Santa in outlines that eventually captured the nation. The dark-clad bishop from Asia Minor was banished for all times in favor of the bulging, booming individual from the Far North.

CHRISTMAS FOR GOD'S CREATURES

Perhaps people in bygone days had closer ties to the earth and its creatures. They were less conscious of their singularity and believed that the dumb animals and plants shared in the joy of humanity on this day of salvation. When the little Christ was born in Bethlehem, not only the Wise Men came to offer gifts; the birds, beasts, and plants came too. In those days cattle in the stable fell down to their knees to worship on Christmas Eve. The ass that was present near the manger figured in most of the mystery plays. Evergreen plants pointed to rebirth of the world in the middle of the winter.

St. Francis of Assisi admonished the farmers to give their oxen and asses extra corn and hay at Christmas, "for reverence of the Son of God, whom on such a night the Blessed Mary did lay down in the stall between the ox and the ass." All creation, said he, should rejoice at Christmas, and the dumb creatures had no other means of doing so than by enjoying more comfort and better food. "If I could see the Emperor," St. Francis said, "I would implore him to issue a general decree that all people that are able to do so, shall throw grain and corn upon the streets, so that on this great feast day the birds might have enough to eat, especially our sisters, the larks."

It is not known when man first used fire in worship and celebrating of joyous occasions. But the ancient Egyptians are known to have done so long, long before the time of Christ. The Persians also used fire, and it was in Persia that the Yule log received its name.

There once each year a tree was felled and a section was cut from the trunk. This section was round and turned like a wheel. It was marked off into four segments representing the four seasons of the year. This calendar-like wheel was called a Yole, and the log from which it was cut was the Yole log. As each season of the year came, the wheel was turned, a great fire was kindled and the Yole log placed in it as the people prayed that their God be kind to them during the coming season.

Blessings

Spring—"May each spring rain shower wealth and prosperity on you all during the coming year."
Summer—"May the bright sun of summer give you strength and health each day during the coming year."
Fall—"May each leaf that falls be a sign of peace and happiness for each of you here as well as the whole world."
Winter—"May the winter wind blow good will and friendship into each heart during the coming year."

Later the Britons adopted the custom and applied it to their Christmas celebration. Here the name Yole gradually became Yule, and here too, the Yule log was carried inside and burned within the house. The barons, lords of the land, threw open their

59

great halls, and all of the people were welcome to enter and join in the festivities as a great fire blazed and leaped on the hearth of the massive fireplace, which often extended across the entire end of the hall.

In preparation for this Christmas celebration a tree had been felled, the log cut, marked, and hidden away in the nearby forest. At a given time the people hurried out in search of it. When it was found, it was carried and dragged joyously to the manor house where it was cut in half and carried into the great hall. There one half was placed upon the fire, and the other half was set aside for use in kindling the fire the following year.

While the log was never used as a religious symbol, it came to be held in respect verging on reverence. Many superstitions grew up around it. Even the ashes were carried away to protect from evil the homes in which they were kept. They were diluted in water and swallowed as cure for internal disorders. They were made into a paste and applied externally for infections.

THE CHRISTMAS CRIB

In churches and homes all over America we find the Christmas Crib constructed with loving care as a part of the decoration or center of special Christmas ceremonies. It was St. Francis of Assisi who first introduced the gentle beasts surrounding the manger. At Christmastide of 1223, he had a farmer of Assisi build a miniature manger. He filled it with straw and had wood carvers make painted figures of the holy Infant and Mother, of ox and ass, and of shepherds and Oriental kings. Then, with Papal permission, he bore it into the church and illuminated it with candles. So Francis raised Christmas—till then only a High Mass—to a festival of love, with worship of the Christ Child shining like a golden light.

The use of the Christmas Crib outside with live animals is also accredited to St. Francis. Three years before his death, he journeyed to Greccio, Italy, to spend Christmas Eve with his old friend Messer Giovanni Velitta. He sent a message about two weeks before Christmas saying:

60

If you desire that we should celebrate this year's Christmas together, go quickly and prepare what I tell you; for I want to enact the memory of the Infant who was born at Bethlehem, and how He was deprived of all comforts babies enjoy; how He was bedded in a manger on hay, between an ass and an ox. For once I want to see all this with my own eyes.

When the Saint of God arrived he found everything prepared. The men and women, as best they could, prepared candles and torches to brighten the night. They sang in praise of God, and the whole town echoed the jubilant outburst. Francis stood before the crib, overcome with devotion and joy, as solemn Mass was sung in front of the manger.

St. Francis was following tradition when he had an ass and ox placed near the manger. The custom originated from a passage in the Old Testament in the words of Isaiah (1:3), "The ox knoweth his owner, and the ass his master's crib; but Israel hath not known me and my people hath not understood." Over the centuries many variations have been added to the Christmas Crib. Always, there is the central group—the Babe in the manger, Mary and Joseph, the shepherds and Wise Men, and the ass and ox on either side.

At the church of Ara Coeli on the Capitaline Hill in Rome is a beautiful statue of the Holy Child. All through the Christmas season it lies in the church crib and is visited by thousands. In front of the crib is a wooden platform where little boys and girls between the ages of five and twelve recite short sermons and poems in honor of the infant Savior. Adults crowd around and listen with rapt attention as the little ones preach to their elders. Visitors to Rome during the Christmas season regard this as one of their most precious experiences because the simplicity and devotion of the little Italian children touches their heart.

Children's Prayer

As the children of Provence, France, kneel in front of the Crib, they say the following prayer:

61

Little Jesus of the crib,
Give us the virtues of those who surround you,
Make us as philosophical as the fisherman,
Carefree as the drummer,
Kind as the ass,
Strong as the ox which keeps you warm,
Give us the sacred leisure of the hunter.
Give us also the desire of the shepherd for earthly things,
The pride of the knife grinder and the weaver,
The song of the miller.
Grant us the knowledge of the Magi,
The cheerfulness of the pigeon,
The impulsiveness of the cock,
The discretion of the snail,
The meekness of the lamb.
Give us the goodness of bread,
The tenderness of the wild boar,
The salt of the haddock,
The good humor of old wine,
The radiance of the candle
The purity of the star.

Nativity Scenes

Since the time of St. Francis, farmers in the mountain areas of Central Europe have spent long winter evenings of Advent repairing and enlarging their beautiful Cribs. The scene is sometimes made up of hundreds of figures, filling an entire room. In many towns there are clubs where children build Cribs of various styles and shapes, using their own imagination and talents. The youngsters are allowed free rein, and there are some utterly charming Cribs as a result.

The custom of building a Nativity scene is practiced in the United States by German-Americans, especially by the Moravians in Pennsylvania and Winston-Salem, North Carolina. They call it "putz" (from the German *putzen*: decorate) and include not only the scene of the Nativity but in addition charming details of a town or countryside. These may depict meadows and fences, windmills that move, lines of soldiers and ponds, etc.

Long thought and effort go into the creation of a putz. Some families have beautiful carved figures which they bring forth every year, while others add new ones each season. There are many versions of the mystic drama, but always there is the central group—the Christ Child in His cradle and the people and animals about Him. On Christmas Eve the family gather around the completed putz with their friends to sing Christmas carols; always included is their beloved "Stille Nacht" or "Silent Night."

In every Catholic Church the world over the same celebration is found in varying degrees. In Alaska, Eskimos come into the missions from frozen wildernesses to see the unveiling of the Nativity. Philippine churches keep their Crib amid a blaze of pink, green, blue, and white candles all during the Christmas season. In India, it is surrounded by tropical ferns, red, pink, and blue flowers, colored streamers, and rich tapestries. The Cribs in Africa and parts of Asia may be made of rough brick against a backdrop of brush, or the American Indian of the plains may make his of straw with a snow-covered roof. Each one, no matter how elaborate or humble, calls to mind the essential meaning of the feast.

Office of the Shepherds

In some churches a little drama takes place as the Crib is unveiled. At Rouen, in France, an ancient mystery play called "Office of the Shepherds" was presented before the beginning of the Midnight Mass and has been described as follows:

The drama commenced when a group of shepherds wearing pastoral costumes made their entrance before the sanctuary. From a height above them an angel sang:
"Fear not for behold I bring you tidings of great joy. . . ."
Other angels from a height chanted:
"Glory to God in the highest; and on earth peace to men of good will."
Hearing this, the Shepherds advanced toward the high altar

63

near which had been erected a Crib. As they approached they sang a hymn of several stanzas:
"Peace on earth is announced, glory in the highest. . . ."
Then they added:
"Let us go to Bethlehem, and let us see this word. . . ."
As they arrived at the Crib two clerics stopped them saying:
"Tell us, shepherds, whom seek ye in the manger?"
"The Savior, Christ the Lord, the Infant wrapped in swaddling clothes," replied the shepherds.
At these words the clerics drew back a curtain from before the Crib and, pointing to the Child that lay within, they sang:
"Here is the little one with Mary, His Mother, of whom Isaiah prophesied long ago."
Then, pointing to the Mother:
"Behold a Virgin shall conceive . . . go and announce that He is born."
The shepherds saluted the Virgin:
"Hail, O privileged Virgin."
Turning to the Child they adored him and announced:
"Alleluia, Alleluia, now we truly know that Christ is born on earth."
As the last notes died away the Mass began and the shepherds took their place to rule the choir.

CHRISTMAS IN AMERICAN CITIES

Most American cities have their own traditional way of saying "Merry Christmas." Since Christmas is an emotional experience, all the old holiday favorites—the Christmas tree and Star of Bethlehem, Santa Clauses on the street, the Salvation Army playing tiny organs and singing familiar hymns, all enhanced by light and color—are brought out every year and never seem to die. Back of all the gaiety is always a memorable spirit of good will to men.

America is composed of many races, and even though many of their traditions are lost in the past, many beautiful customs are revived during the Christmas season. Just so, our great American cities are made up of many heritages, and their Christmas cele-

64

brations are as individual and different as the racial strains of the people. We have searched the files of the National Recreation Association for past celebrations of cities throughout the country and selected ones that might be adapted for use in a small community or church for a Christmas celebration.

A Modern Bethlehem

At the turn of a switch each year, the mining town of Madrid, New Mexico, is a modern Bethlehem. Not much is heard of Madrid most of the year, but late in the afternoon of December 24 a great change comes over it, and the roads leading to it are clogged with cars, with carts, with cowboys on horses and pilgrims afoot. As the procession approaches, trees light up throughout the village, and the lovely strains of "Silent Night, Holy Night" break the silence. Suddenly the little church is bathed in light and the Bethlehem scene reenacted. As darkness descends, figures and scenes of the first Christmas are suddenly floodlighted against the pine and cedar hills just twenty miles south of Santa Fe. Bowers of decorated arches and miles of sparkling, living Christmas trees appear under tall lighted candles and thousands of electric lights. The story of the birth of Christ is told in huge dioramas and oil paintings, one of which measures thirty-three feet. Following the story in paintings, one sees Mary and Joseph leave Nazareth to go to Bethlehem, the Nativity scene, the shepherds on the hillside outside the walled city, the search of the Wise Men, and the flight of the Holy Family from Bethlehem. From over the hills, powerful machines bring the angels' message, and the strains

65

of "Noel," "Silent Night, Holy Night," "O Little Town of Bethlehem," and "It Came Upon A Midnight Clear" drift down on the scene from hidden amplifying systems.

All this started over forty years ago when a few miners, who were tired of the dreary coal-dusty atmosphere of their camp, set out a few evergreens in their yards and hung them with lights. There were only a dozen or so the first year; the next there were twenty-seven; now there are thousands. Each year the celebration has grown, and though for the first five years it was a hometown affair, thousands of visitors come to work on the various displays and to help the miners to renew the spirit of Christmas.

The Birds' Christmas Tree

A quietly sheltered little nook of trees and vines known as "The Bird Sanctuary" is in a clump of native growth adjacent to the Garden Center Building of the nationally famous Fort Worth Botanic Garden. It is at Christmastime that a graceful elm out in front lifts its gaily decorated branches up into the air so the birds, too, might have a happy Christmas.

Strings of brilliant white popcorn garlands make it a truly old-fashioned tree. Scarlet cranberries glisten invitingly as they sway in the wind. Fat red apples reign atop the sturdier branches, and on the lowest limbs tidbits of bread are served by sturdy toddlers.

For fun in preparation, and to make the tree gayer, some ingenious groups fashion original figures of edibles. One tubby little Saint Nick may flaunt a cheese slab head, have features of raisins and sunflower seed, a doughnut tummy, legs of toast, and arms of alternately sturdy cranberries and tiny round cereals. Individual feeding trays are made from sturdy cups with ample feeding openings cut in the sides, holding bits of broken peanuts and pecans and crumbs of stale cake. Clever suet logs offer the birds' favorite fare of peanut butter, alongside meal and bacon grease balls and globs of health-giving suet. Grain and chick-scratch are scattered beneath the sheltering boughs for the ground-feeding birds.

When the decorating is through, there is a feast for the birds for Christmas and many other days, and the boys and girls stand back and look with awe and satisfaction on their project, which, in ever so subtle a manner, has quickened compassion and conservation in their hearts.

Christmas In Hawaii

Hawaii has its own natural Christmas decorations—festive poinsettias and red, waxy blooms on byways to decorate homes and churches.

A Matson freighter, nicknamed the "Christmas Tree Ship," comes each year with a stock of fir trees from the United States Northwest. Arriving about the same time on the beach at Waikiki is Santa himself. Whether he surfs in on a board or paddles to the sand in a canoe is immaterial to the children. From that moment the streets are filled with people singing carols to the accompaniment of ukuleles.

A Christmas Gift to the People

The Lansing, Michigan, federal orchestra, the Michigan State College a cappella choir, and the Lansing's Civic Players Guild joined forces for a community Christmas program at the Prudden Auditorium, sponsored by the Recreation Department. The participating organizations called their concert "a Christmas gift to the people of Lansing," and a delightful gift it proved to be! The a cappella choir sang English, Catalonian, and Mexican carols; the federal orchestra presented Saint Saens' "Carnival of the Animals," and the production of the Players Guild was the "Saint" with offstage music by the girls' choir of Plymouth Congregational Church. Community singing was a part of the program.

"Christmas Carols Are for Everyone"

For over fifty years St. Louis has given America its—and perhaps the world's—greatest program of carol singing, heard annually today by thousands of people. The observance began almost by accident, when in 1911 nine people went out to sing before the houses of friends. The response was so warm that they

67

continued their caroling calls the following year and the year after that. The first year a number of people, greatly moved by the music, had reached into their pockets and handed money to the nine singers. "Give it to a good cause," the listeners told them. The carolers contributed the fifty dollars to a group of St. Louis children's organizations—a first gift that would grow to thousands each year in years to come.

Seattle's Christmas Ship

There's no more fitting place in the world for Santa Claus to take to the water. That's the way Park Superintendent Paul V. Brown felt about Seattle back in 1949, and it was in his office that the idea for Seattle's famous Christmas originated. The ship sailed that very Yuletide, carrying its lighted Christmas tree and caroling crew along miles of the city's fresh and salt water shoreline.

Cruising slowly through the lakes and the Ship Canal, the 106-foot yacht *Valkyrie* presented a gala picture in her role as Christmas ship. The sleek white hull and deck houses were garlanded with colored lights, and a tall Christmas tree glowed amidships. An orchestra and chorus serenaded the uncounted thousands who gathered at vantage points along the shore.

The Christmas ship was a true community project. Narman Berg, owner of the *Valkyrie*, donated her services free of charge.

Oil firms provided fuel, crew members served without pay for the most part, while the Coast Guard and other boat owners formed a colorful escort fleet. Labor and material for the decorations and loudspeaker system were taken care of by the city lighting department and the parks department, while public-spirited citizens and business firms contributed the cash needed for incidental expenses.

An International Christmas

In Dayton, Ohio, Bamberger Center decided to prolong the day by having "Twelve Days of Christmas," with a different foreign Christmas represented for each of the twelve days. Nationality groups in the city agreed to participate in the festival, and each, in turn, chose one of the days to present their Christmas. Features in the program included folk dancing, traditional carols, holiday foods, native costumes, and talks on appropriate customs.

A Christmas Candelabra

In Fort Worth, Texas, a huge Christmas tree in Burkburnett Park is chosen as the site for a unique Christmas celebration. It is the setting for a huge candelabra of fifty electric candles which becomes the Christmas symbol of community loyalty and good will. The double-tiered triangle of lights measures eighteen feet wide and eight and a half feet from the metal base to the top of the tallest candle. As the date of the candle-lighting ceremony draws near, forty-nine religious, cultural, civic, educational, and other organizations cooperate in the program, and each selects a representative for the pageant. The citizens are coached in their parts, the park is put in readiness, thousands arrive for the ceremony, and the candle lighting begins. When the representative of each group is introduced to the people, he pulls the switch which lights his candle and then gives a half-minute Christmas greeting from his particular organization.

When the forty-nine greetings have been offered, the mayor of the city lights the center candle, which towers above the others, and brings a message from the city of Forth Worth.

Christmas Cheer Week

Christmas Cheer Week—the week between Christmas and New Year's—has become a well-loved tradition in Salt Lake City, Utah, and each night a special program is given. It was as a result of this program that the Salt Lake City Opera Company was organized. In addition to opera, the Salt Lake Civic Orchestra presents a sacred Christmas program two days before Christmas in cooperation with the choir of one of the churches.

On Christmas Eve, Salt Lake City has a tree lighting service on the Community Building grounds when the mayor wishes everyone a "Merry Christmas." The program is broadcast and thousands of trees troughout the city are lighted simultaneously with the community Christmas tree. All the carol groups of the city assemble at the tree lighting service and begin their caroling there.

Each year on the day before Christmas the Recreation Department's Harmonica Band presents a program. The children, some 150 strong, assemble at the City and County Building and play several carols on their harmonicas. From this point they go to the hotels and one or two of the department stores and give a carol program. Later in the week they visit hospitals and institutions where the spectators enjoy the delight of the children in performing for them.

Largest Nativity Scene

Anyone living within a few hundred miles of Bethlehem, Pennsylvania, should make a pilgrimage there to see the beautiful Nativity scene, or *putz,* as the Moravians call it. A huge star, visible for twenty miles, stands aloft South Mountain to greet the visitors. It is a permanent fixture, one hundred feet in height, with hundreds of glistening lights. The official city seal is in this same star, the five points representing the city's major interests: religion, music, industry, recreation, and education.

The beautiful putz is unveiled on Christmas Eve. The following statistics give an idea of its size and the work involved in constructing it. One year the Crib required 800 pounds of sand, 12 bushels of moss, 64 stumps of trees, 40 Christmas trees, 48 angels,

200 animals, including sheep, camels, and leopards, 16 lighting effects, 29 lamps, 700 feet of rock earth, 400 feet of various other materials, and several paintings in oil. The putz varies yearly, but the theme is the same.

Largest Living Christmas Tree

For many years Wilmington, North Carolina, has claimed the largest living Christmas tree in the world. A giant water oak, said to be three hundred years old, stands more than seventy-five feet high and has a diameter of one hundred feet, making a shining hill of green leaves and moss in Hilton Park above the Cape Fear River. Most of Wilmington's Christmas centers on the town's great tree. The lights, numbering over five thousand, are turned on during the week before December 25, and the tree remains illuminated until January 1. Bands play, choral groups sing, and night after night there are musical programs. Thousands of people visit the live oak and marvel at this great spectacle created by God and man.

Fort Myers' Singing Christmas Tree

It begins to look a lot like Christmas in Fort Myers, Florida, when members of the Fort Myers High School Glee Club take part in their annual Singing Christmas Tree ceremony. The members form an animated tower in one of the parks, and a hundred young voices tell the Christmas story in pageantry and song. Some of the Glee Club members form a living tableau on either side of the tree. On one side are the Three Kings of the Orient; on the other the shepherds in their field. High above, on the tree, is the Star of Bethlehem to guide them to the Christ Child.

The color combinations are as much a part of the presentation as the voices of the singers. Those who make up the "tree" are clad in dull gold gowns with a Christmas-green collar. Clasped hands hold green wreaths of holly, bright with crimson berries. Brilliant poinsettia plants deck the stage, and holly boughs practically cover its edges. Florida Power and Light Company sparks the tree into a spectacle of shining light.

71

Charlotte Singing Christmas Tree

Charlotte, North Carolina, has a world-famous Singing Christmas Tree that stands inside the Ovens Auditorium. The voices that come from the "tree" are those of the Charlotte Choral Society, 115 a cappella performers, who sing to a three-day audience of over 100,000 people.

The tree is twenty-seven feet, eight inches high and is made up of a number of 150-pound portable sections which require over a thousand bolts to hold them in place. At the very top stands a live evergreen that brings the total height to at least thirty-two feet.

Since the members of the Charlotte Choral Society are all adults with highly trained voices, the program is classical rather informal. It includes carols, art songs, and great liturgies of the

𝒯he Charlotte Choral Society
𝒜nd 𝒯he Charlotte Observer 𝒫resent
THE SINGING CHRISTMAS TREE
FOR THE BENEFIT OF OBSERVER CHARITIES

𝒫rogram

I
THE JOYOUSNESS OF THE MIDDLE AGES

Voix Celestes _____ Gilbert A. Alcock
A Ceremony Of Carols _____ Benjamin Britten

II
THE MYSTERY OF CHRISTMAS

Sleepers, Wake! A Voice Is Sounding _____ J. S. Bach
The Three Kings _____ Healey Willan
Love Came Down At Christmas _____ Garth Edmundson
Did Mary Know? _____ Richard E. Averre
Christ Is Born _____ Ukranian Carol
                                    Arr. by Robert M. Boberg

III
THE LEGEND OF CHRISTMAS

The Holly And The Ivy _____ Traditional English
                                    Arr. by Salli Terri
Mexican Christmas Procession _____ Mexican Christmas Carol
                                    Arr. by Paul Christiansen
Touro-louro-louro _____ Provencal Carol by Nicolas Saboly
                        Arr. by Alice Parker—Robert Shaw
Here, Mid The Ass And Oxen Mild   Traditional French
                        Arr. by Alice Parker—Robert Shaw
Do You Hear What I Hear? _____ Noel Regeny—Gloria Shayne
                                    Arr. by Harry Simeone

INTERMISSION

IV
A CHILD'S DREAM OF CHRISTMAS

Prayer From "Hansel And Gretel" _____ Engelbert Humperdinck
                                    Arr. by Wallingford Riegger
Five Nursery Rhymes _____Arr. by Ralph Hunter
    1. Humpty Dumpty
    2. Little Bo-Peep
    3. Little Jack Horner
    4. Mary Had A Little Lamb
    5. Old King Cole
The Rock-a-by Lady   Michael Colina
It Came Upon The Midnight Clear_____ Alice Parker—Robert Shaw
The First Nowell _____ Alice Parker—Robert Shaw

73

V
PEACE ON EARTH AMONG MEN OF GOOD WILL

Sweet Little Jesus Boy _____ *Robert MacGimsey*
                Charles Higgins, Tenor
Mary Had A Baby _____ *Negro Spiritual*
                            Arr. by Charles Black
Christmas Spiritual _____ *Charles Higgins*
Behold That Star _____ *Thomas W. Talley*
                            Arr. by Frank Cunkle
Sister Mary Had But One Child _____ *Setting by Roland Hayes*
                Charles Higgins, Tenor
Go Tell It On The Mountain _____ *Christmas Spiritual*
                            Arr. by John W. York
He's Got The Whole World In His Hands
          Text Selected and Arranged by Charles Higgins
There Is A Balm In Gilead _____ *William L. Dawson*
Let There Be Peace On Earth _____ *Sy Miller—Jill Jackson*
                            Arr. by Hawley Ades

church. We are including their 1966 program of dramatic Christmas music for two reasons: first, as a guide for selecting classical Christmas music and, second, because records have been made of most of the songs. They are available in both stereo and monaural and may be purchased from the Charlotte Choral Society, 519 Fendor Place, Charlotte, North Carolina.

CHRISTMAS LEGENDS, ESPECIALLY FOR CHILDREN

The Christmas Angel

Every Christmas, so the story goes, the Blessed Mary selects a number of angels and sends them down to earth in various parts of the world. Each angel awakens a little child from its first sleep and carries it to heaven to sing a carol to the Christ Child. When

the children afterward tell of their beautiful errand, some people will say it was just a dream; but others will assure you that these children are chosen by God to be blessed with unusual favors in this life and with great glory in the next.

Legend of the Pine Tree

When the little Christ Child was born in Bethlehem, not only the Wise Men came to offer gifts; the birds, beasts, and plants came too. Each had something to offer the little Jesus, excepting the pine tree. It had nothing to give except its needles, and they would only prick the Baby and were not at all suitable. But God saw how disappointed the little tree was, and told some of the stars to go down and rest on its branches. When they did, the little tree was covered with such radiance that when the Child saw it, He stretched out His arms toward it in happiness. From that time forth, at Christmas time, the little pine tree always bears lights which we place there in memory of the night it gave pleasure to the Christ Child.

Robin Red Breast

An old French legend has a pleasing explanation of how the robin got its gaudy chest. It seems that on Christmas night an early bird used its wings to fan the fire that kept the Christ Child warm as He lay in the manger. The glowing heat of the flames kept the robin's breast red forever.

Legends of Christmas Flowers

White Rose. Madelon, a little girl, followed the shepherds on their way to Bethlehem. But when she saw that everyone brought presents, she hesitated sadly. One of the announcing angels saw her distress and waved her lily over the winter-barren ground, which came alive with white Christmas roses. Madelon collected them and brought them to the Child, who turned away from the gold of the Wise Men to stretch His hands toward the lovely flowers.

Chrysanthemum. Another legend tells of the birth of the chrys-

75

anthemum on Twelfth Night. When the Magi had reached the village of Bethlehem to which the star guided them, they looked around in vain for a sign of a great event. Everything was quiet. All the houses seemed asleep, so they did not know which one to enter. Suddenly King Melchior bent down as he saw a strange flower shaped like the star itself. When he picked it, the door of the stable opened by itself.

The Rosemary. This fragrant plant has been connected with Christmas since time immemorial. According to an old legend, it was honored by God in reward for the humble service it offered to Mary and her Child. On the way to Egypt, so the charming story goes, Mary washed the tiny garments of Jesus and spread them over a rosemary bush to dry in the sun. Since then the rosemary has delighted man by its delicate fragrance and spicy flavor.

Flower of Bethlehem. This delicate white flower is found in almost every country in the world. It is said that the star that shone so brightly in the night and guided the shepherds to the manger where the Christ Child lay had fulfilled its purpose. It broke into little pieces and scattered over the fields as white blossoms. Joseph went out at dawn and gathered them to bring back to his family.

Poinsettia. This beautiful flower with its burning red leaves and a center of yellow pods which we see at Christmastime is called "Flower of the Holy Night" in Mexico. A charming Mexican legend explains its origin:

On Christmas Eve long ago, a poor boy went to church in great sadness, because he had no gift to bring the Holy Child. He dared not enter the church and, kneeling humbly on the ground outside, prayed fervently and assured our Lord with tears how much he desired to offer Him some lovely present. "I am very poor and dread to approach the Babe with empty hands." Just then he saw, springing up at his feet, a green plant with gorgeous blooms of dazzling red. He broke some of the beautiful flowers from the plant and joyously entered the church to lay his gift at the feet of the Christ Child. Since then the plant has spread over the whole land, and we in this country call it the Christmas flower, symbolic of the Savior's birth.

CHRISTMAS CAROLS

The word "carol" originally referred to a dance accompanied by the playing of flutes. These dances or singing games were usually done in ring form to musical words that indicated the actions. The dancers would form a circle and, joining hands, walk in a rhythmic dance while keeping the shape of a circle.

In the modern sense, a hymn is essentially solemn; a carol, gay and joyful. Following the restoration of Christmas in England, there were numerous festive songs in praise of the Feast, but very few religious carols. One of the few was the ballad "While Shepherds Watched." Early religious carols employed both rhyme and alliteration, such as the tender lullaby songs sung by the Virgin Mary.

Christmas carols are numerous—so much so they can be under many headings according to subject. The largest group are the Nativity carols, followed by star carols, shepherd carols, mystery

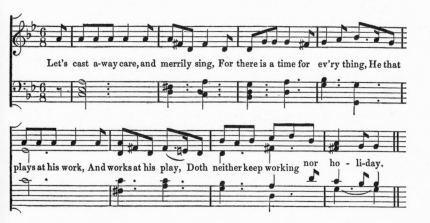

Let's cast a-way care, and merrily sing, For there is a time for ev'ry thing, He that plays at his work, And works at his play, Doth neither keep working nor ho - li-day.

THE WAITS

Some of the tunes which the waits of different towns played, are contained in *The Dancing Master* of 1665 (among the violin tunes at the end), and others in *Apollo's Banquet*, 1669. The York Waits seem to have chosen a hornpipe tune, which was printed in broadsides, with words by Mr. Durden. From these the following are selected, as descriptive of the custom in that city, about the end of the 17th century :—

" In a winter's morning,
Long before the dawning,
Ere the cock did crow,
Or stars their light withdraw,
Wak'd by a hornpipe pretty,
Play'd along York city,
By th' help of o'ernight's bottle,
Damon made this ditty, ...
In a winter's night,
By moon or lanthorn light,
Through hail, rain, frost, or snow,
Their rounds the music go ;
Clad each in frieze or blanket
(For either heav'n be thanked),
Lin'd with wine a quart,
Or ale a double tankard.
Burglars scud away,
And bar guests dare not stay,
Of claret, snoring sots
Dream o'er their pipes and pots,
Till their brisk helpmates wake 'em,
Hoping music will make 'em

To find the pleasant Cliff,
That plays the Rigadoon.
  *   *   *   *
Candles, four in the pound,
Lead up the jolly Round,
Whilst cornet shrill i' th' middle
Marches, and merry fiddle,
Curtal with deep hum, hum,
Cries, we come, we come, come,
And theorbo loudly answers,
Thrum, thrum, thrum, thrum, thrum.
But, their fingers frost-nipt,
So many notes are o'erslipt,
That you'd take sometimes
The Waits for the Minster chimes :
Then, Sirs, to hear their music
Would make both me and you sick,
And much more to hear a roopy fiddler call
(With voice, as Moll would cry,
" Come, shrimps or cockles buy"),
" Past three, fair frosty morn,
Good morrow, my masters all."

The following was composed by Jeremiah Savile, and is on the last page of Playford's *Musical Companion*, 1673, entitled THE WAITS :—

The following is called *The Waits* in *The Dancing Master* of 1665, and *London Waits* in *Apollo's Banquet*, 1663 :—

LONDON WAITS

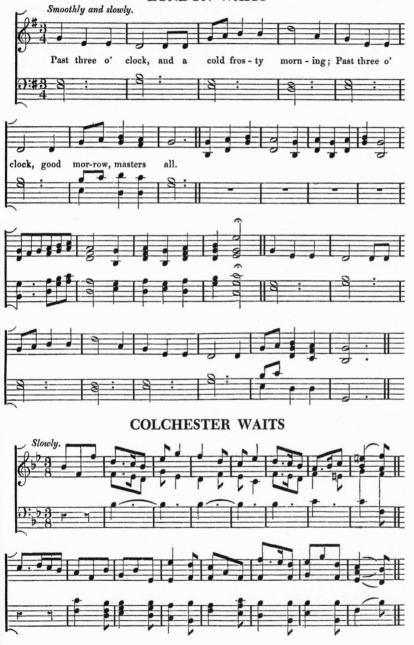

Smoothly and slowly.

Past three o' clock, and a cold fros-ty morn-ing; Past three o'

clock, good mor-row, masters all.

COLCHESTER WAITS

Slowly.

GREEN GROW THE LEAVES

—Northants (R. S. Baker).

Green grow the leaves on the hawthorn tree,
Green grow the leaves on the hawthorn tree,
We jangle and we wrangle and we never can agree,
But the tenor of our song goes merrily, merrily, merrily,
The tenor of our song goes merrily.

—R. S. Baker (*Northants Notes and
Queries*, ii. 161).

BABE OF BETHLEHEM

Hexatonic, mode 4 a (I II — IV V 6 7)

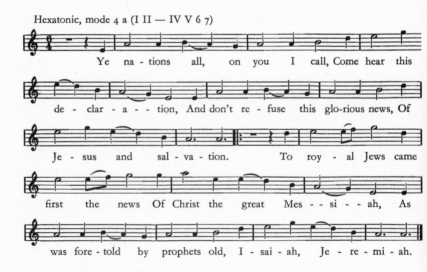

Ye na - tions all, on you I call, Come hear this
de - clar - a - - tion, And don't re - fuse this glo-rious news, Of
Je - sus and sal - va - tion. To roy - al Jews came
first the news Of Christ the great Mes - - si - - ah, As
was fore - told by prophets old, I - sai - ah, Je - re - mi - ah.

80

To Abraham the promise came,
And to his seed forever,
A light to shine in Isaac's line,
By scripture we discover;
Hail, promised morn, the Savior's born,
The glorious Mediator —
God's blessed word made flesh and blood,
Assumed the human nature.

His parents poor in earthly store,
To entertain the stranger
They found no bed to lay his head,
But in the ox's manger;
No royal things, as used by kings,
Were seen by those that found him,
But in the hay the stranger lay,
With swaddling bands around him.

On the same night a glorious light
To shepherds there appeared,
Bright angels came in shining flame,
They saw and greatly feared;
The angels said, "Be not afraid,
Although we much alarm you,
We do appear good news to bear,
As now we will inform you.

"The city's name is Bethlehem,
In which God hath appointed,
This glorious morn a Savior's born,
For him God hath anointed;
By this you'll know, if you will go
To see this little stranger,
His lovely charms in Mary's arms,
Both lying in a manger."

When this was said, straightway was made
A glorious sound from heaven,
Each flaming, tongue an anthem sung,
"To men a Savior's given,
In Jesus' name, the glorious theme,
We elevate our voices,
At Jesus' birth be peace on earth,
Meanwhile all heaven rejoices."

Then with delight they took their flight,
And wing'd their way to glory,
The shepherds gazed and were amazed,
To hear the pleasing story;
To Bethlehem they quickly came,
The glorious news to carry,
And in the stall they found them all,
Joseph, the Babe, and Mary.

carols, etc. There are also the dance carols for the usual ring dances accompanied by singing. We have included as many types of carols as space will allow.

The Waits

Among the musicians who furnished music for Old English Christmas celebrations were the *waits*. They seem to have been a kind of watchman who, in order to prove their watchfulness, were required to pipe or sing at given hours during the night. They are described as having blue gowns with red sleeves and caps. Everyone had about his neck a silver collar. We suggest the following wait songs or ditties for use in a dramatic production to denote periods of time or in between episodes or acts in a play:

English Song and Ballad Music

In Bethlehem, in Jewry, this blessed babe was born,
And laid within a manger, upon this blessed morn;

81

Tho which his mother Mary did nothing take in scorn.
O tidings, &c.

From God, our Heavenly Father, a blessed Angel came,
And unto certain Shepherds brought tidings of the same,
How that in Bethlehem was born the Son of God by name.
O tidings, &c.

Fear not, then said the Angel, let nothing you affright,
This day is born a Savior of a pure Virgin bright,
To free all those who trust in Him from Satan's pow'r and might.
O tidings, &c.

The Shepherds at those tidings rejoiced much in mind,
And left their flocks a feeding, in tempest, storm, and wind,
And went to Bethlehem straightway, this blessed babe to find.
O tidings, &c.

But when to Bethlehem they came, where our dear Savior lay,
They found Him in a manger where oxen feed on hay;
His mother Mary, kneeling unto the Lord did pray.
O tidings, &c.

Now to the Lord sing praises, all you within this place,
And with true love and brotherhood each other now embrace;
This holy tide of Christmas all others doth deface.
O tidings, &c.

A CHRISTMAS LOVE FEAST

The Moravian Love Feast commemorates a Christmas Eve over
two hundred years ago when a little group of missionaries gathered in a log cabin in Pennsylvania's wilderness to celebrate the
birthday of the Prince of Peace. In its group was Count von Zin-
zendorf, who had come to Pennsylvania in the hope of uniting
various religious groups.

During the evening's devotions, the Count was deeply im-
pressed with the similarity of their shelter, housing both men and
beasts, to that in which Jesus was born in the City of David. Im-

GOD REST YOU, MERRY GENTLEMEN

Moderate time.

God rest you, mer-ry gen-tle-men, Let no-thing you dis-may; For Je-sus Christ, our Sa-vi-our, Was born on Christ-mas-day, To save us all from Sa-tan's pow'r, When we were gone a-stray: O tid-ings of com-fort and of joy, comfort and joy, O tid-ings of com-fort and of joy.

In Bethlehem, in Jewry, this blessed babe was born,
And laid within a manger, upon this blessed morn ;
The which his mother Mary did nothing take in scorn.
> O tidings, &c.

From God, our Heavenly Father, a blessed Angel came,
And unto certain Shepherds brought tidings of the same,
How that in Bethlehem was born the Son of God by name.
> O tidings, &c.

Fear not, then said the Angel, let nothing you affright,
This day is born a Saviour of a pure Virgin bright,
To free all those who trust in Him from Satan's pow'r and might.
O tidings, &c.

The Shepherds at those tidings rejoiced much in mind,
And left their flocks a feeding, in tempest, storm, and wind,
And went to Bethlehem straightway, this blessed babe to find.
O tidings, &c.

But when to Bethlehem they came, where our dear Saviour lay,
They found Him in a manger where oxen feed on hay ;
His mother Mary, kneeling, unto the Lord did pray.
O tidings, &c.

Now to the Lord sing praises, all you within this place,
And with true love and brotherhood each other now embrace ;
This holy tide of Christmas all others doth deface.
O tidings, &c.

A VIRGIN MOST PURE

A Christmas Carol still sung in the West of England, taken from Mr. Sandys's
Collection. The tunes of this and other Carols are not exclusively appropriated to
the words with which they are here united; various Carols are sung to each air.

84

In Bethlehem city, in Jewry it was,
Where Joseph and Mary together did pass,
And there to be taxed, with many one mo',
For Cæsar commanded the same should be so.
            Rejoice and be merry, &c.

But, when they had entered the city so far,
The number of people so mighty was there,
The King of all Glory to the world being
            brought,   [wrought;
Small store of fine linen to wrap him was
When Mary had swaddled her young Son so
            sweet,
Within an ox manger she laid him to sleep.
            Rejoice, &c.

Then God sent an Angel from heaven so high,
To certain poor Shepherds in fields where they
And bid them no longer in sorrow to stay, [lie,
Because that our Saviour was born on this day.
            Rejoice, &c.

That Joseph and Mary, whose substance was
Could get in the city no lodging at all. [small,
            Rejoice, &c.
Then they were constrain'd in a stable to lie,
Where oxen and asses they used to tie ;
Their lodging so simple, they held it no scorn,
But against the next morning our Saviour was
born.   Rejoice, &c.
Then presently after, the Shepherds did spy
A number of Angels appear in the sky,
Who joyfully talked, and sweetly did sing,
To God be all Glory, our Heavenly King.
            Rejoice, &c.

Three certain Wise Princes, they thought it
            most meet
To lay their rich off'rings at our Saviour's feet ;
Then the Shepherds consent, and to Bethlehem
            did go,
And when they came thither, they found it
            was so.   Rejoice, &c.

pulsively, he seized a lighted taper and led the way where the cattle were kept, singing the while an old German Epiphany hymn, "Not Jerusalem, Lowly Bethlehem." Thus, the occasion suggested the name of Bethlehem for their new settlement.

Every Christmas the Moravians around Bethlehem and Winston-Salem, North Carolina, usher in the holidays with their celebrated Love Feast to the accompaniment of their famous trombone choir, which announces all festival days as well as the passing away of members of the congregation. The Love Feast begins in the afternoon of Christmas Eve, primarily for the children of the congregation. They sit in a body at the front of the church, which is pleasantly fragrant with evergreen decorations. After the congregation has sung several hymns, the Love Feast, always consisting of a sweet bun and cookies along with a steaming beverage, is served by the sacristans to each child. Toward the close of the service, the sacristans and assistants return, this time with trays of lighted beeswax candles. The tapers, casting a soft glow on bright, happy faces are held in the children's hands until the benediction has been pronounced.

After the service there is an interval for a family celebration in the home. But at seven thirty, the congregation reassembles for the Christmas Eve Vigil. After the church is packed, the lights

85

THE FIRST NOWELL

A Carol for the morning of Christmas Day; the tune from Mr. Sandys' Collection.

Gracefully.

The first Now - ell that the an - gels did say, Was to cer - tain poor shep-herds in fields as they lay, In fields where they lay, keep-ing their sheep, On a cold win - ter's night that was so deep. Now - ell, Now - ell, Now - ell, Now - - ell, Born is the King of Is - ra - el.

are dimmed, with the exception of one lighted star hanging in the center and over a picture of the Holy Family. Then begins the most beautiful service of the year, a service devoted almost exclusively to music, performed sometimes by the Bach choir, some-

86

NOBE'S MAGGOT (WHIM OR FANCY)

In *The Dancing Master* of 1703, this is entitled *Nobe's Maggot*. In *The Devil to Pay* another version is named *There was a maid in the West*.

There are many tunes of this class, closely resembling each other in character, and sometimes in actual notes.

Gaily.

O   you mer - ry souls, Christ-mas is   a   coming, We shall have flow-ing bowls,

Dancing, pip- ing, drumming,   De - li -cate minc'd pies,   For   to feast each vir - gin,

Ca-pon and   goose, likewise   Brawn and a dish   of   stur - geon.

Then, for your Christmas-box,
    Sweet plum-cakes, and money,
Delicate Holland smocks,
    Kisses sweet as honey.
Hey for the Christmas ball,
    Where we shall be jolly,
Coupling short and tall,
    Kate, Dick, Ralph, and Molly.

Then to the hop we'll go,
    Where we'll jig, and caper
Cuckolds all a row ;
    Will shall pay the scraper :
Hodge shall dance with Prue,
    Keeping time with kisses ;
We'll have a jovial crew
    Of sweet and smiling misses.

times by children, and sometimes by the congregation. At one point a child chosen from the Sunday School sings antiphonally with the other children that hymn which, to every Moravian, is the keynote of the Christmas season:

Morning Star, O cheering sight!
Ere Thou cam'st how dark earth's night!
Jesus mine, in me shine;
Fill my heart with love divine.

87

REMEMBER, O THOU MAN

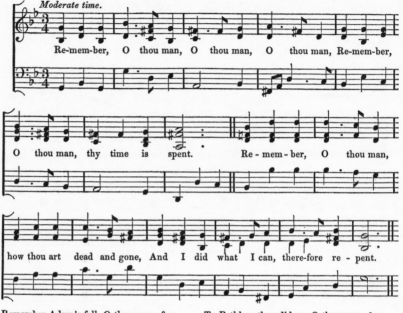

Moderate time.

Re-mem-ber, O thou man, O thou man, O thou man, Re-mem-ber, O thou man, thy time is spent. Re - mem - ber, O thou man, how thou art dead and gone, And I did what I can, there-fore re - pent.

Remember Adam's fall, O thou man, &c.,
  Remember Adam's fall, from heaven to hell;
Remember Adam's fall, how we were con-
  demned all
In hell perpetual there for to dwell.

Remember God's goodness, O thou man, &c.,
  Remember God's goodness and his promise
  made;   [Son, doubtless,
Remember God's goodness, how he sent his
Our sins for to redress;—Be not afraid.

The angels all did sing, O thou man, &c.,
  The angels all did sing upon the shepherd's
  hill;   [King,
The angels all did sing praises to our heavenly
And peace to man living, with a good will.

The shepherds amazed were, O thou man, &c.,
  The shepherds amazed were, to hear the
  angels sing;   [come to pass
The shepherds amazed were, how it should
That Christ, our Messias, should be our
King.

To Bethlem they did go, O thou man, &c.,
  To Bethlem they did go, the shepherds
  three;   [so or no,
To Bethlem they did go, to see wh'er it were
Whether Christ were born or no, to set man
free.

As the angels before did say, O thou man, &c.,
  As the angels before did say, so it came
  to pass;   [babe where it lay,
As the angels before did say, they found a
In a manger, wrapt in hay, so poor he was.

In Bethlem he was born, O thou man, &c.,
  In Bethlem he was born for mankind's sake;
In Bethlem he was born, for us that were
  forlorn,   [take.
And therefore took no scorn our flesh to

Give thanks to God always, O thou man, &c.,
  Give thanks to God always with heart most
  joyfully;   [day—
Give thanks to God alway, for this our happy
Let all men sing and say, Holy, holy.

CHRISTMAS CAROL

The Burden or Chorus.

Now - ell, nowell, now - ell, nowell, [Now-ell, now-ell, now - ell.] This
Bring us in good ale, good ale, And bring us in good ale:

is the sa - lu - ta - tion of the an-gel Ga - bri - el. Ti-dings true there
For our bless-ed La-dy's sake, bring us in good ale. Bring us in no

be come new, sent from the Trin - i - ty, By Ga - bri - el to Na - za - reth,
brown bread, for that is made of bran, Nor bring us in no white bread, For

ci - ty of Ga - li - lee: A clean maiden and pure virgin, Through her hu-mi-li -
there - in is no gain. But bring us in good ale, good ale, And bring us in good

-ty . . Hath con-cei-ved the per - son second in De - i - ty.
ale. For our blessed La-dy's sake, Bring us in good ale.

ᵃ The two bars marked off by a line are added, because there would not otherwise be music enough for the *Was-sail Song*. They are a mere repetition of the preced-ing, and can be omitted at pleasure. The only way in which the latter could have been sung to the music as written in the manuscript, would be by omitting the line " And bring us in good ale;" but, as it is *merely* a repe-tition, it *could* be omitted.

ALL YOU THAT ARE GOOD FELLOWS

In marching time.

All you that are good fel - lows, Come heark-en to my song; I know you do not hate good cheer, Nor li-quor that is strong. I hope there is none here, But soon will take my part, See - ing my mas - ter and my dame Say wel - come with their heart.

This is a time of joyfulness,
  And merry time of year,
When as the rich with plenty stor'd
  Do make the poor good cheer.
Plum-porridge, roast beef, and minc'd pies,
  Stand smoking on the board;
With other brave varieties,
  Our master doth afford.

Our mistress and her cleanly maids
  Have neatly play'd the cooks;
Methinks these dishes eagerly
  At my sharp stomach looks,
As though they were afraid
  To see me draw my blade;
But I revenged on them will be,
  Until my stomach's stay'd.

Come fill us of the strongest,
  Small drink is out of date;
Methinks I shall fare like a prince,
  And sit in gallant state:
This is no miser's feast,
  Although that things be dear;
God grant the founder of this feast
  Each Christmas keep good cheer.

This day for Christ we celebrate,
  Who was born at this time;
For which all Christians should rejoice,
  And I do sing in rhyme.
When you have given thanks,
  Unto your dainties fall,
Heav'n bless my master and my dame,
  Lord bless me, and you all.

Near the close of the service, the doors on the front of the church open. As the choir begins to sing, "Behold! A great and heavenly light, from Bethlehem's manger shineth bright," the sacristans enter with trays of lighted candles as at the Love Feast. This time the entire congregation is served with candles which transform the church into a veritable sea of light.

Moravians spent weeks in preparation for the Love Feast, pouring beeswax into molds that were used by their ancestors. Paper frills of various colors are placed around the base for decorative purposes and to prevent the hot wax from hurting those who hold the candles.

Moravian Cookies

Moravian Christmas cookies are of two kinds: one a light sugar cookie and the other made of a dark dough containing dark molasses. They are cut into traditional shapes and used for tree decorations. Brown cookies should be cut into shapes of men, birds, dogs, sheep, roosters, and other animals. Light cookies should be cut into semblances of stars, angels, hearts, trees, and flowers.

NEW YEAR'S

In the minds of many people Christmas and New Year's come together as if they had something in common. Actually, of course, this is not true. Christmas is a deeply religious holiday, whereas New Year's Day does nothing more than mark the beginning of the civil year. Like many of our festivals, it probably had its origin with the Romans, who celebrated January 1 in honor of Janus Befors, a god with two faces. One face always looked back to the old year and the other looked forward. He was the keeper of heaven and earth; in his right hand was a key with which he locked a gate which closed the old year and opened the new. In his left hand was a scepter, a symbol of power.

The Old New Year

Of New Year's Day Charles Lamb said that no one, of whatever rank, can regard it with indifference. "Of all sounds, of all bells," he said, "most solemn and touching is the peal which rings out the New Year. I never hear it without a gathering up of my mind to a concentration of all images that have differed over the past twelve months; all I have done or suffered, performed or neglected, in that regretted time. I begin to know its worth when a friend dies. It takes a personal color."

Forgive Me . . . for the New Year

To many people New Year's Day provided an occasion for closing rifts and healing disputes; as much as anything else, it was a day of reconciliation. It was as much a custom to greet a person with "Forgive me for the New Year" as to say, "Happy New Year." Even if there had not been a misunderstanding, one friend would greet another by shaking hands and saying: "If I have done you any wrong during the year just past, I want you to forgive me for the new one."

Visiting Day

In the 1840's and for years thereafter, New Year's was the visiting day for the men and receiving day for the ladies. Callers began to arrive as early as ten o'clock in the morning, as they had many rounds to make before nightfall. On a stand in the hall was a silver tray in which a few calling cards from last year's stock were placed so that the first caller might not be embarrassed by the fact that he was first. No one was invited—the humblest man had the right to hand in his card at the door, walk in, and partake of the refreshments. These usually consisted of an immense decorated cake, placed on a table in the parlor, and beside it a great bowl of eggnog. Scattered about the room were little cornets of bonbons, dragées, and cornucopias filled with nuts.

The Gay New Year

Today everyone resolves to make the coming year better than the year that has just passed into eternity. Generally it is a day of rejoicing, and people go from house to house wishing everyone a "Happy New Year." Many churches conclude the Christmas season with some kind of service, and often a party follows. Sometimes the service will take the form of Holy Communion, and people may make vows and commitments regarding the New Year. The General Commission on Evangelism of the Methodist Church has published an additional *Office of Worship for New Year's Eve*. It may be used by an individual in solitude, by families and groups of friends, by youth groups waiting for the New Year, or by a congregation at a Watch Night Service.

On New Year's Eve there are many parties with singing and dancing. There always seems to be some mystery in the air that keeps people awake until twelve o'clock for fear they will miss something. Just before midnight everyone stands as their glass is being filled. Then, suddenly, the moment arrives—everyone toasts the New Year, shakes hands and kisses each other, and again wish all a "Happy New Year." The party breaks up slowly, and as it ends, everyone joins in singing

"Should auld acquaintance be forgot . . ."

Ringing Out Of The Old Year

Ring out, wild bells, to the wild sky,
The flying clouds, the frosty light;
The year is dying in the night;
Ring out wild bells, and let him die.

Ring out the old, ring in the new,
Ring happy bells, across the snow;
The year is going, let him go;
Ring out the false, ring in the true.

Ring out the grief that saps the ming
For those that here we see no more;
Ring out the feud of rich and poor,
Ring in redress to all mankind.

Ring out a slowly dying cause,
And ancient forms of party strife;
Ring in the nobler modes of life,
With sweeter manners, purer laws.

Ring out the want, the care, the sin,
The faithless coldness of the times;
Ring out, ring out my mournful rhymes,
But ring the fuller minstrel in.

Ring out false pride in place and blood,
The civic slander and the spite;
Ring in the love of truth and right,
Ring in the common law of good.

Ring out the old shapes of foul disease;
Ring out the narrowing lusts of gold;
Ring out the thousand wars of old,
Ring in the thousand years of peace.

Ring in the valiant man and free,
The largest heart, the kindest hand;
Ring out the darkness of the land,
Ring in the Christ that is to be.

Alfred Tennyson

NEW YEAR'S IN OTHER LANDS

In most countries the New Year Festival is the most important holiday of the year; in some it is a day of merriment, but in others it is an occasion of solemnity and prayer. Most ancient nations celebrate the New Year with the coming of spring, but in India, the Hindus celebrate the first day of each of the four seasons. The date on which we celebrate our New Year (January 1), like the

94

THREE MERRY MEN OF KENT

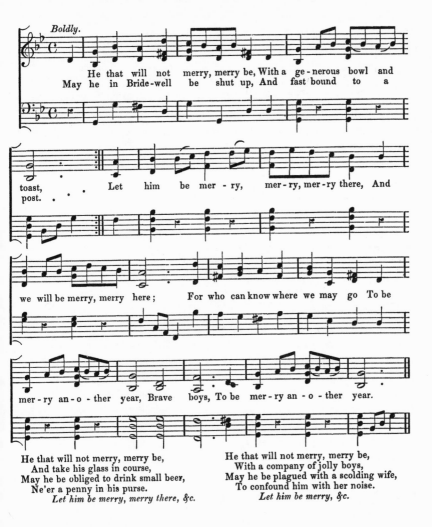

Boldly.

He that will not merry, merry be, With a ge-nerous bowl and
May he in Bride-well be shut up, And fast bound to a

toast,
post.
   Let him be mer - ry, mer-ry, mer-ry there, And

we will be merry, merry here; For who can know where we may go To be

mer - ry an - o - ther year, Brave boys, To be mer-ry an - o - ther year.

He that will not merry, merry be,
And take his glass in course,
May he be obliged to drink small beer,
Ne'er a penny in his purse.
Let him be merry, merry there, &c.

He that will not merry, merry be,
With a company of jolly boys,
May he be plagued with a scolding wife,
To confound him with her noise.
Let him be merry, &c.

date of Christmas, is inherited from the Romans. It was Julius
Caesar who changed the date from March to January in honor
of Janus, the god of all beginning.

Jews all over the world celebrate Rosh Hashonoh (Jewish New
Year) at the end of summer, close to the autumn equinox. The
holiday is sometimes called "The Day of the Sounding of the
Ram's Horn"—the call from the Heavenly Shepherd to listen to the

THREE LITTLE SHIPS

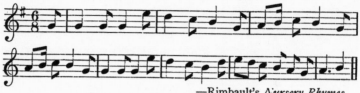

—Rimbault's *Nursery Rhymes.*

I. Three little ships come sailing by,
    Sailing by, sailing by;
    Three little ships come sailing by,
    New Year's day in the morning.

Who do you think was in the ships,
    In the ships, in the ships;
Who do you think was in the ships,
    New Year's day in the morning?

Three pretty girls were in the ships,
    In the ships, in the ships;
Three pretty girls were in the ships,
    New Year's day in the morning.

One could whistle, and one could sing,
    One could play on the violin;
One could whistle, and one could sing,
    New Year's day in the morning.
                            —London (A. B. Gomme).

II. I saw three ships come sailing by,
     Come sailing by, come sailing by;
     I saw three ships come sailing by
     On New Year's day in the morning.

And what do you think was in them then,
    In them then, in them then;
And what do you think was in them then,
    On New Year's day in the morning?

Three pretty girls were in them then, &c.

One could whistle, and one could sing,
    The other could play on the violin;
Such joy was there at my wedding,
    On New Year's day in the morning.
                            —Rimbault's *Nursery Rhymes.*

Voice of God. On this day the Book of Life is opened, and good and evil acts, words and thoughts of each person, are examined.

Japan

The greatest day of this nation is the New Year. Debts are paid —a moral, not a legal obligation, but a custom so strongly rooted that people unable to meet their financial obligations hide themselves in shame. On New Year's Eve, adults stay up for the night watch gong to ring at midnight. It sounds 108 times to purge the 108 human weaknesses described in Buddha's teachings.

Four Direction Worship. The New Year opens at the Imperial Sanctuary at four o'clock in the morning with "worshiping in four directions." The Emperor looks toward heaven and earth, the hills and stars, in all four directions. He asks that peace may reign in the country and abundant crops grow during the coming year.

New Year's Ode Party. In the month of January every year, the New Year's Ode Party is held in the presence of the Emperor and Empress at Court, with many dignitaries in attendance. The theme of the ode is imposed by the Emperor toward the end of the previous year, and any person can send a short poem of thirty-one syllables that he or she may compose on the given subject. For instance, the theme one year was "Snow on the Farmhouse." The judges are appointed by the Emperor in January, and poems they select are announced at the meeting along with those of the Emperor and Empress and members of the Court. The reading begins with the poems submitted by nonofficials and courtiers of lower rank, followed by courtiers of higher rank, and so on up to members of the imperial family.

Chinese New Year

The Chinese New Year is primarily a family festival when men return to their homes to pay respect to their ancestors, to perform their religious duties, to greet the elder members of their clan, and to enjoy a well-earned rest after a year's hard work. Then, too, New Year's is also a birthday celebration for every Chinese, for regardless of the actual date on which a Chinese child is born, he is considered exactly a year old on New Year's Day. Just as in Japan, men go out early in the day to settle their debts, for the New Year must be faced with a clean slate.

The Chinese New Year begins the first day of the first full moon, which means anytime between January 21 and February 19. This fourteen-day festival is celebrated in all Chinese cities and villages and in large American cities that have an area known as "Chinatown." On each day a special theme is carried out, ending with the greatest celebration of the year, The Feast of Lanterns.

At midnight members of a family present New Year wishes to one another. The master and mistress seat themselves in a chair in the reception hall where all those living under the same roof appear and k'o t'ou before them. In this ceremony the order of seniority is strictly observed.

On this first day, also, it is customary for ancestors to receive offerings and prayers. Even distant relatives, when visiting, are led to the domestic altar to do reverence. The last baby of the family will be carried there in its mother's arms and taught to bow his tiny head, which is dressed in a holiday cap with little figures of the eighteen Buddhist saints in gold, silver, or copper.

The second day ends the family reunion, and the streets are filled with merrymakers. Neighbors and friends bow to each other and present New Year wishes. On the third day a home service to Tsai Shên, the God of Wealth, is held. His pictures are found in most Chinese homes and shops, and each year they are burned and replaced by new ones.

On the fourth day of the New Year, everyone who has a decent coat pays a call upon relatives and friends, taking care when he leaves his home for the first time in the New Year to choose a lucky spot for his first footstep. During the next ten days other special themes are celebrated, but it is customary for children to go from house to house singing holiday songs and waiting for doors to open so they can receive rice cakes or some kind of fruit. All during the season, too, roving bands of actors present plays and pageants on a holiday theme, usually relating to the dragon.

Feast of Lanterns. On this last day of the New Year celebration, all China is aglow with thousands of gaily decorated lanterns. The lanterns are made in all colors and shapes. To attract prosperity and longevity, people attach them to fir branches and hang them above their doors. The peasants put up poles dressed in long strings of lanterns outside the temples, giving the effect of tents of light.

The Feast of Lanterns may be regarded as preeminently the holiday season for children. For several days bands of young village boys dress up in strange costumes and go about by day and night acting little plays, partly in dumb show, partly in speech. Some of them wear terrifying masks of wild beasts; others are in girls' clothing. At night they carry large lighted lanterns and march amid music and song in procession along the streets.

In the United States, we are more familiar with the dragon that goes up and down the street demanding alms or being destroyed. He has a large papier-mâché head to which is fastened a long red velvet train ornamented with embroidery and jewel-like sparklers. A dozen or more men form the legs of the dragon by getting under the train, and the two men in front hold the head high with their arms and hands. A man leads the way by beating vigorously on a drum.

Diwali—Indian New Year

Diwali, the Feast of Lights, is the final night of a Hindu autumn festival. One of the most picturesque and well known of Indian observances, it is almost universally celebrated, although the customs vary in different parts of the country. All observances of Diwali, however, have one common feature, profuse illumination. Tiny clay saucers are filled with mustard oil in which homemade cotton wicks float. The small lights, called *chirags*, are placed on the edge of roofs and window ledges and are set in rows along river banks and driveways.

The purpose of the lighting is to guide Lakshmi, the goddess of prosperity, to every house to distribute her gifts. In south India pipers and drummers visit each celebrating house, beginning

99

about 3:00 A.M., play a few numbers, and then move on. Next morning they always return to demand money or gifts.

Africa

In the Ethiopian calendar, New Year's Day comes the first week in September. Children gather flowers on New Year's Eve and make them into small bunches. Singing and dancing, they call on neighboring homes. If the householder responds with a gift, he or she is rewarded with a nosegay. If he does not (which is unusual), the children depart with sad faces and their flowers.

Syria and Lebanon

New Year's Day is the time for merrymaking. It is then that gifts are exchanged and children go from door to door with New Year's greetings and, in turn, are given candy and small coins. Syrian children believe the camel is the bearer of gifts rather than Santa Claus. Before going to bed on New Year's Eve, they put out a bowl of water and a dish of wheat for the camel. Legend says that this camel was the youngest of those that carried the Three Wise Men to see the Christ Child and that it fell down exhausted by the long journey. But the Christ Child blessed the camel and conferred immortality on it.

Norooz—New Year's Day in Iran

Norooz, or New Year's Day, is the big festival of the year in Iran. This national holiday, which falls at the spring equinox, March 21, not only marks the beginning of the New Year but also heralds the arrival of spring. It is believed that each person should be as happy as possible when the New Year arrives. It is the custom to pop a piece of candy into everyone's mouth while a passage from the Koran is read in Moslem homes.

New Year's dinner is celebrated by the family sitting around a tablecloth spread out on the floor on which are placed a number of symbolic objects. Among them is an egg and a mirror, both of which have a special and very interesting significance. Legend says that the earth trembles slightly as it begins a new year. At the right and precise moment, the egg is placed on the mirror. To everyone's intense delight the egg always trembles a bit—perhaps the rumble and vibrations of cannons which go off at the same instant to proclaim the arrival of the New Year help matters.

Why People in Taiwan Say, "Kiong-hee" at New Year's

Before there were electric lights or even kerosene lamps in Taiwan, lamps were made from lengths of bamboo. The hollow bamboo was filled with oil, and wicks were made of soft twists of cotton threads. These were called "monkey lamps."

The ancients had a ceremony of making little rice-flour balls and placing them all over things in their houses on New Year's Eve. They would put them on tables and chairs, on the beds and cupboards, on the stoves, on the doors, and even on lamps. One New Year's they forgot the monkey lamps which made the spirits very angry. They said: "On earth people are very bad. Rice-flour balls are very carelessly used. Destroy the people!"

When the king of heaven heard of man's ingratitude he said, "Ingratitude is indeed unforgiving. Mankind shall be destroyed. I'll send a great flood on New Year's Eve and drown them all."

On New Year's Eve the people gathered around their fires, family by family. They wore their best clothes, ate a fine dinner, and talked of the happiness that had been theirs. There was great sadness that all was going to end the next day.

Now the kitchen god was very close to the people. When he heard them talk like this, he went straight to the king of heaven and said, "You must not destroy the people. If anyone knows what they are like, it is I. I see them every day. The people are not wicked."

The kitchen god explained that the people were very busy that night thanking all the spirits with their flour-rice balls—they just forgot the monkey lamps. "Anyone can make a mistake." The king knew the kitchen god was reliable and so he forgave them. But the people went solemnly to their beds, not knowing their fate had been changed.

Next morning, New Year's Day, one man slowly and fearfully opened his eyes. He was still in his own room with his wife lying on the wooden bed beside him. He shook her awake.

"Kiong-hee, congratulations! You are alive!"

The wife sat up with a start. "Why, so I am! And so are you! Kiong-hee!"

She ran from room to room, waking up every member of the family with, "Kiong-hee! You're alive!"

On that and each succeeding New Year in Taiwan, the people greet each other with "Kiong-hee," congratulations.

JANUARY 6—EPIPHANY OR TWELFTH NIGHT

January 6 is a holiday of many moods—to some it merely means the end of the Christmas season, but for many it has a deeper meaning. To most churches it is known as "Epiphany" and is the close of the Christmas cycle. The popular meaning of the holiday in America is the Adoration of the Magi when they came to Bethlehem to see the Christ Child.

The name "Epiphany" comes from a Greek word meaning "appearance" or "manifestation." The purpose of the festival, then, is to commemorate the manifestation of the Son of God to man. The Greek Church holds that the Epiphany celebrates Christ's baptism by John the Baptist and also two other events—the miracle of Cana in turning water into wine and the feeding of the five thousand, both of which are said to have occurred on this date.

Adoration of the Magi

To most Americans, particularly children, January 6 means Twelfth Night or the anniversary of the night the Three Wise

102

Men were guided to Bethlehem by a blazing star in the winter sky. It was Henry Wadsworth Longfellow who popularized the story in his poem *The Three Kings*.

Three Kings came riding from far away,
    Melchior, and Gaspar, and Balthazar;
Three wise men out of the East were they,
And they traveled by night and they slept by day.
    For their guide was a beautiful, wonderful star.

.   .   .

And the Three Kings rode through the gate and the guard,
    Through the street till their horses turned
And neighed as they entered the great inn-yard;
But the windows were closed and the doors were barred,
    And only a light in the stable burned.

And cradled there in the scented hay,
    In the air made sweet by the breath of kine,
The little child in the manger lay,
The child that would be King one day,
    Of a kingdom not human but divine.

The Three Wise Men were considered to have been royal personages, but the names Melchior, Gaspar, and Balthazar must come from the annals of history and not from the Bible. They were the first of the heathen world to do homage to Christ. According to legend, *Melchior* was an old man with white hair and a long beard. He brought gold in testimony of Christ's royalty. *Gaspar* was young, beardless, and of ruddy hue. His gift of frankincense was a token of His divinity. *Balthazar* is pictured as black of complexion with a heavy beard. The myrrh he held in his hands prefigured the death of the Son of God.

There is a legend that after many years had passed the Magi were visited by St. Thomas, the Apostle, who after instructing them in Christianity baptized them. They were then ordained to priesthood and later made bishops. It is said that once more the Star of Bethlehem appeared to them and reunited them at the end of their lives. The city of Sewa in the Orient is given as the place of their burial. The legendary relics of the Magi were brought to Constantinople in the fifth century; one hundred years later they were transferred to Milan, and in 1164 to Cologne under Emperor Barbarossa. Their shrine was, and still is, the center of many pilgrimages.

The Star Song

Robert Herrick, during the first half of the seventeenth century, wrote *The Star Song* to be sung at White Hall. Since then it has become legend in English Christmas festivals, and we are including the poem with the suggestion it be used as a special feature in a Twelfth Night service:

The Star Song—A Carol to the King

Tell us, thou clere and heavenly Tongue,
Where is the Babe but lately sprung?
Lies he the lily banks among?

Or say if this new birth of ours
Sleeps, laid within some ark of flowers
Spangled with dew lights? Thou cans't cleere
All doubts, and manifest the where.

Declare to us bright star, if we shall seek
Him in the morning's blushing cheek,
Or search the beds of spices through,
To find him out?

Star

No, this we need not do:
But only come, and see Him rest
A princely Babe in's mother's breast.

Chorus

He's seen! He's seen! Why then around
Let's kiss the sweet and holy ground
And all rejoice that we have found
A King before conception found.

104

Come then, come then, and let us bring
Unto our prettie Twelfth-Tide King
Each one his several offerings.

And when night comes wee'l give him wassailing;
And that his treble honors may be seen
Wee'l chuse him King and make his mother queen.

Celebrations by Greek Orthodox Church

January 6 is recorded in the Greek Orthodox Church as an ancient celebration of an event in the life of Christ which is considered as the beginning of His official dedication to His divine mission to man. The celebration is called "Epiphany"—a combined Greek word which is derived from *epi* and *phainein,* to show or shine upon. The feast includes the birth of Jesus Christ, His baptism, and the appearance of the Father and the Holy Spirit.

The Sanctification of the Waters

On both days, the fifth and sixth of January, the Service of the Blessing of the Waters on the Epiphany takes place. After the Matins and Divine Liturgy, the priest comes forth in the center of the nave (many times outside the church) to the vessel of clean water. It is a solemn Procession when the people or the choir sings the prelude hymn:

The voice of the Lord crieth upon the waters: Come, receive ye the Spirit of wisdom, the Spirit of understanding, the Spirit of the fear of God, of the manifested Christ.

"Let us attend" the deacon cries, "let us attend to hear the prophecy, the Wisdom of God." And the reader reads three parts from Isaiah beginning with 35:1, 55:1, and 12:3.

Thus saith the Lord: the wilderness and the solitary place shall be glad; and the desert shall rejoice, and blossom as the lily. The desert of Jordan shall blossom abundantly . . . and

105

my people shall see the glory of the Lord, and the excellency of our God. . . .

And straightway, after blessing the waters with the sign of the cross, the priest immerses the sacred cross upright in the water and raises it again, intoning the following dismissal hymn:

When Thou, O Lord, was baptized in Jordan, the worship of the Trinity was manifest. The voice of the Father bore witness to Thee, calling Thee His Beloved Son; and the spirit in the form of a dove, confirmed the immutability of the words. Thou hast appeared, O Christ our God, and hast illuminated all the world; glory to Thee.

The full text of this celebration may be purchased in pamphlet form from OLOGOS, P.O. Box 5333, St. Louis 15, Missouri.

In some cities and towns the custom prevails that the people go after the service in a solemn procession to the nearby rivers or seashores where the priest throws the cross into the waters. Divers are awaiting to recover the cross from the waters and return it to the priest.

After the service, the faithful receive sanctified water and take it home and reverently drink of it and sprinkle it around their homes and fields, reciting the dismissal hymn.

Feast Of Lights

The celebration of the Feast of Lights is not held as a commemoration of a historical event, but merely for the attraction of lights, music, and poetry. It is a remembrance that Christ is ever present and His Grace is not merely a memory of history. The priest intones:

Holding torches and candles in our hands and with our voices and feelings of devotion, together we raise a symbol to *the living Christian God—the Holy Trinity*, the Father and the Son and the Holy Spirit—as He appeared at the moment of the Baptism of Jesus Christ, as He has been determined by the Church in the Creed, as He is accepted by every living

106

Christian, as the living God, the God who harkens to our voices, the God Whom we beseech to accept us in communion, whom we hope to have as our Companion, who is our Comforter, Who is Alpha and Omega of our Faith. To Him, with fear and love we dedicate the day.

Twelfth Night Revelry

Down with the Rosemary, and so
Down with the Baies and mistletoe:
Down with the Holly, Ivie, all,
Wherewith ye drest the Christmas Hall:
That so the superstitious find
No one least Branch there left behind:
For look, how many leaves there be
Neglected there (maids trust to me)
So many *Goblins* you shall see.

Robert Herrick

Plundering The Christmas Tree

To young people Twelfth Night marks the end of the Christmas season, and the prevailing spirit is that of carnival. It is an old belief that one way to bring good luck to the home for the coming year is to keep the Christmas greens until the Feast of Epiphany, or January 6. Christmas trees were left standing with all their decorations until that evening, when the plundering of the tree began. After sundown, people wishing to take part in the celebration would meet and go from house to house where they would dance around the tree and partake of the last of the Christmas goodies.

In anticipation of the arrival of guests, the hostess would remove all ornaments from the tree, together with the polished fruits and the candies that had been wrapped in brightly colored tin foil, and place them in small piles around the room. When the guests arrived they were allowed to choose the pile that had the greatest appeal for them, and the candy and fruit were served as refreshments. The tree ornaments were taken home and carefully

107

stored away until next year, when they were used to decorate the new trees.

After each home had been visited, all the plundered Christmas trees were carried to the center of the town and burned. The celebration ended around the bonfire, and one might imagine everyone singing the last stanza of *Gather Around the Christmas Tree*.

Farewell to thee, O Christmas tree!
Farewell to thee, O Christmas tree!
Thy part is done
And thy gifts are gone,
And thy lights are dying one by one:
For earthly pleasures die today,
But heavenly joy shall last always,
Hosanna, hosanna, hosanna in the highest!

GATHER AROUND THE CHRISTMAS TREE

King of the Bean

There is also the ancient and honorable ceremony of the "crowning of the King of the Bean," who reigned supreme during Twelfth Night and was allowed to choose a lady to be his Queen. This custom probably originated in France, although it was also practiced in England and Scotland.

The French king would invite members of his court to assemble on Twelfth Night to elect a King of the Bean by acclamation. Everyone, including the servants, was allowed to vie for the honor. First the jugglers stepped before the king and performed their most difficult feats; the minstrels played and sang their choicest music; the court jester told his favorite jokes; and even the gentlemen and ladies in waiting entered the contest by performing in plays or telling stories. The person who received the greatest applause was crowned King of the Bean and clothed in a scarlet robe. He reigned during the evening.

The Twelfth Cake

In England no "Little Christmas" was complete without a Twelfth Cake. There cakes were generally made of pastry and baked in a large round pan like a pie. A bean was baked into it, and whoever found the bean in his cake became king and led the festivities during the evening.

Mary Queen of Scots Party

At the age of six, Mary Queen of Scots was sent to France to be educated in her mother's country, and with her went three little girl companions. They were known as the "Four Marys," because the given name of each of them was Mary.

One Twelfth Night, Mary Queen of Scots had a King of Bean party in Holyrood, and Mary Flemming drew the bean. The story goes that Queen Mary allowed her to dress in clothes selected from her wardrobe and permitted her to rule in her place for the day.

4. EASTER CYCLE

Easter was the first Christian high holiday, coming into existence very early in the history of Christianity at a time when the death and resurrection of Christ were more important than his birth. In the beginning, Easter was a season rather than day, but early in the sixth century a definite time was set for the festival. It is a movable feast that begins on the first Sunday after the full moon crosses the vernal equinox. This is the point where the sun crosses the celestial equator about March 20 every year, making day and night of equal length everywhere.

To all Christians, Easter is the greatest day on the church calendar because it celebrates our Lord's greatest miracle—His Resurrection. This movable feast covers a forty-day period. Actually, there are more than forty days between Ash Wednesday and Easter Sunday, but since Sunday is always a feast day, only weekdays are counted. The festival is divided into three parts:

Lent—a preparation of our Lord's Passion
Holy Week—includes Palm Sunday, Maundy Thursday, Good Friday, and Holy Saturday
Easter Sunday—the week following is called "Week of Renewal" because of the great restoration accomplished by the Resurrection.

110

To some people the spirit of the pre-Lenten season is one of penance, devotion, and prayer. Others have a more worldly aspect of the season familiarly known to us as carnival. The best-known celebration of carnival in America is the famous Mardi Gras in New Orleans, which takes its name from the day on which it is held. Similar celebrations are also held in other cities and towns of Louisiana, Florida, and Alabama.

It is during this season that two Christian celebrations are held —World Day of Prayer and Brotherhood Week. Both are days of worship without denominational, racial, national, or cultural distinction, and each has assumed greater importance each year as churches become more liberal in their thinking.

World Day of Prayer

The Mighty One, God the Lord, speaks and summons the earth from rising of the sun to its setting:

> Come with comfort of His Love abiding;
> Come with the sense of His Grace, divining;
> Come with the knowledge of His Wisdom, plenteous;
> Come with the sureness of His Power, endless;
> Come with the joy of His Presence, radiant;
> Come with the hope of His Promises, certain;
>   And abide in prayer.

This was the call in 1955 to women all over the world to join in a World Day of Prayer. The Presbyterian Church in the United States first proposed a national day of prayer in 1887, and other denominations soon followed suit. In 1919 women began to observe it, and today an organization is sponsored by the United Church Women of the National Council of Churches.

The World Day of Prayer falls on the first Friday in Lent, when the sun crosses the International Date Line in mid-Pacific, carrying the prayers of millions of women westward as the sun makes its orbit. Each year special prayers come from a different country —in 1966, they came from Scotland.

111

Truly worldwide in character, the same worship service is used in 125 countries and areas in the world as evidenced by the following reports:

In Bermuda, "It was a dreadful night of wind and rain. We held the service in the evening to suit those who work or have babies. It took courage to face the elements . . ."

"A sawdust-burning stove heated the building comfortable," a correspondent from Korea wrote.

Realizing that they formed a link in a chain around the world, Polish women prayed and thanked God for the unity of Christians.

A group of African women wrote a poem for the service:

> Come everybody, come everybody,
> Prepare to come to the house of God.
> Come, come, come—
> The hour of worship is near,
> Prepare your bodies, prepare your hearts.
> Come, come, come.

Each year a different theme is chosen for the day, and special pamphlets are prepared by United Church Women for the celebrations. Groups wishing to take part in the service may purchase the pamphlets for a nominal fee. In addition to these materials a film strip, "That Friday," is available in sound and color, telling of the concern of women all over the world. It may be ordered along with other material from United Church Women, National Council of Churches, 475 Riverside Drive, New York, N.Y. 10027.

Brotherhood Sunday

Brotherhood Sunday is officially celebrated in all religious institutions on the Sunday nearest Washington's Birthday. However, in recent years, it has been extended to Brotherhood Week with many organizations scheduling programs through the entire month of February. The celebration is designed to help different religions understand each other and to discuss problems that di-

112

In any forest there are many different trees. But each tree draws sustenance from the same earth & reaches upward to the same GOD

vide the different faiths. The thesis of the program is based on George Washington's admonition that "the privilege of worshiping God in any way one wishes was both a choice blessing and a precious right of the people."

The Brotherhood movement places special emphasis on youth programs. It urges youth organizations to meet with similar groups of other religions, not to worship but for social periods and discussions of civic concerns. During the month, it is customary for city churches to exchange with pastors of other faiths to officiate at the morning service. St. George Episcopal Church in New York City exchanged their whole congregation with one in Harlem.

Brotherhood Week is sponsored by the National Conference of Christians and Jews. This organization was founded in 1928 by Charles Evans Hughes, Newton D. Baker, and S. Parks Cadman, joined by Carlton J. H. Haynes and Roger W. Straus. Any church desiring literature or program material may write to the National Conference or contact their own city branch. The address of the national headquarters is 43 West 57th Street, New York, N.Y. 10019.

113

Taking Leave of Alleluia

Alleluia, meaning "Praise the Lord," is a hallowed exclamation of joy in all church liturgy. On Septuagesima Sunday (the third Sunday before Lent) the Alleluia is officially discontinued in all Catholic churches to signify the approach of the solemn season of Lent.

Since the time of Pope Alexander II (1060) the Alelluia has been sung twice after the Divine Office and not heard again until the solemn Vigil Service of Easter, when once more it is used as a glorious proclamation of Easter joy. All organs are silent during the same period.

Christian churches all over the world include the Alleluia in all their Easter services in praise of the Risen Lord. The word also inspired Handel's familiar Halleluia Chorus in his oratorio "The Messiah."

LENT

The word Lent is of Anglo-Saxon origin, meaning spring, but to Christians it is a forty-day period of self-examination and repentance in preparation for the Easter festival. There are several reasons for the forty-day season—to commemorate the forty days Moses spent on Mount Sinai, the forty years wandering, the forty days Jesus spent in the desert, or the forty hours in the tomb. To most people it is a period of strengthening their fath in the Lord, through the media of repentance and prayer.

For almost a thousand years the Catholic Church followed a norm laid down by Pope Saint Gregory the Great for fasting during the Lenten season: "We abstain from flesh meat and from all things that come from the flesh as milk, cheese, eggs and butter." Among the Eastern Catholic Churches and in the Greek Orthodox Church in America, people still retain the old strict routine. According to a new ruling of the Ecumenical Council in Rome, Roman Catholics are obligated to fast on only two days during Lent— Ash Wednesday and Good Friday.

To most Christians, Lent is a period of quietness and medita-

tion symbolizing the ancient words of Jesus to the tired activist:
"Come, ye, into the desert and rest a while." For people burdened
by many responsibilities and sometimes confused decisions, a few
weeks of quiet contemplation help to renew strength and deepen
insights into world problems.

Because of the solemnity of the season, church programs become richer and more meaningful than at any other time of year.
This is the result of the conviction of most members that during
Lent they should reduce their social programs and give more time
time to private prayer and service in the community. In many
churches ministers are inclined to preach a series of sermons of a
doctrinal nature A common theme is the Seven Last Words uttered on the Cross, the first Divine Pulpit of Christianity:

"FATHER, forgive them; for they know not what they do."
(Luke 23:34)
"WOMAN, behold thy son! . . . behold thy mother."
(John 19:26, 27)
"VERILY I say unto thee, to-day shalt thou be with me in Para-
dise." (Luke 23:43)
"MY God, my God, why hast thou forsaken me?"
(Mark 15:34; Matthew 27:46)
"I thirst." (John 19:28)
"IT is finished." (John 19:30)
"FATHER, into thy hands I commend my spirit." (Luke 23:46)

Protestant Churches celebrate Lent in a number of ways. Most
denominations hold Holy Communion on each Sunday, and many
churches make a special offering daily in the chapel as a service to
the public. It is the custom in some churches to organize special
Bible study classes for children and adults. The Episcopal Church
uses the penitential office which is found in the Book of Common
Prayer. Almost every church sets aside its usual Sunday evening
services for cantatas, oratorios, and other presentations of Lenten
and Passion music.

Ash Wednesday

Ash Wednesday marks the beginning of Lent for Catholics of the Latin rite as well as some Protestant Churches. On this day priests will repeat the admonishment, "Remember, man, that thou art dust and unto dust thou shalt return," as they place the mark of the cross of ashes on foreheads of the faithful.

The ashes are made from the branches of brushwood or palms which were consecrated the previous year on Palm Sunday. They are sifted, cleaned, and given a special blessing before they are distributed on Ash Wednesday. The custom of strewing ashes on the head in the form of a cross is a sign of humility and penance.

Mothering Sunday (Fourth Sunday in Lent)

This charming custom originated in England where, on the last Sunday in Lent, boys and girls who lived away from home were allowed to go back to the Mother Church in which they had been baptized or brought up. They carried with them gifts to place in front of the altar. The Mother prefix means "home or refuge," thus the origin of the term "Mother Church," "Mother's Day," and an old saying: "He who goes a-mothering finds violets in the lane."

The Sunday is also celebrated according to the popular meaning of the word, much as Mother's Day is observed in America. Young people who live away from home return on that day to visit their mothers. Those in domestic service are given a holiday, and the returning boys and girls do the chores.

Laetare Sunday

The fourth Sunday in Lent is also called Laetare Sunday. As a symbol of joy for the day (Mid-Lent), the Popes used to carry a golden rose in their hand while celebrating Mass. Originally it was a single rose of natural size, but since the fifteenth century it has consisted of a cluster or branch of roses made of pure gold and set with precious stones. The Pope blesses it every year and often confers it upon churches, shrines, or dignitaries as a token of esteem. In case of such a bestowal, a new rose is made during the subsequent year.

An adaptation of this Papal custom is Notre Dame's annual award (since 1888), a medal of award to an American lay Catholic who has distinguished himself in science, literature, philosophy, or sociology. The medal is made of heavy gold and black enamel tracings.

HOLY WEEK

Holy Week celebrates the last days in the life of Christ and recapitulates those events that have had particular significance in shaping the Christian religion. There was a time when these sacred days were to be free from worldly occupation and the entire week devoted to religious exercises. But later, when conditions changed, the church decided to hold the services in the evening for benefit of those who work and retain only Good Friday as a Holy Day. As time went on, the week preceding Easter was developed as a very special preparation for the festival and the week that followed as a special time of rejoicing. The Catholic Church has a complete Missal, "The Sacred Triduum of Holy Week" for services on Holy Thursday, Good Friday, and Easter Vigil. Protestants observe Holy Week, each in their own way, without a set ritual. Most churches hold services in the evening with appropriate music and sermons. Sometimes special services are held each noon hour, and a visiting pastor of prominence is engaged to give the meditation.

Palm Sunday

Palm Sunday commemorates the entry of Jesus into Jerusalem as described by Saint Matthew:

117

He entered the city riding on an ass, and multitudes spread their garments in the way; others cut down branches of trees and strewed them in the way. Crowds cried, "Hosanna to the Son of David."

From very early days, Christian churches have ordered that branches be carried in procession on that day. Palms are usually used for branches (hence the name of Palm Sunday), but other trees are also used. Many European countries carry willow branches or pussy willows bearing their catkin blossoms. Sometimes two twigs are joined to form a cross, and men wear them in their hats.

In Protestant churches palms are often distributed to the congregation and a special sermon and music prepared for the occasion. In Catholic churches a service called the "Blessing of the Palms," which includes a number of superb prayers relating to imagery of the palms, is observed. During the morning Mass, a history of the Passion according to Saint Matthew is sung by three clerics vested in white albs and black stoles. The chant is a solemn and beautiful melody in different pitches. One (tenor) represents the evangelist; the second (high tenor) chants the voices of different people and crowds; and the third (bass) sings only the words of Christ.

Domingo de Ra
(Palm Sunday in the Philippines)

The blessing of the young coconut palms on Palm Sunday is one of the most beautiful folk Catholic traditions that has been handed down during the four hundred years of Philippine Catholic history. The ceremonial is for the most part a children's affair. The custom is based on the antiphons "Pueri Habraeorum," which are sung during the distribution of the palms:

> The Hebrew children bear-
> ing branches of olive,
> Went forth to meet the Lord,
> crying out

And saying: Hosanna in the
highest!

The Hebrew children spread
their garments along the
way,
And cried out saying: Hosanna to the Son of David,
Blessed is He who comes in
the name of the Lord.

The little boys cut the white young palm branches from any accessible coconut tree on the Saturday before Palm Sunday. They then weave the pliant stalks into various intricate and artistic designs of birds, flowers, elaborate crosses, etc. These preparations go on all Saturday afternoon, for every little boy in town is expected to carry a coconut palm branch to church the next day, Sunday.

The Angels. The little girls have a different preparation to make. Out in the churchyard, the men of the parish are preparing two or three well-decorated platforms called *bahay-bahayan,* from which little "Angels" will throw a shower of flowers after Mass next day. The little "Angels," girls between the ages of six and twelve, also are busy all Saturday afternoon gathering flowers and getting ready their white dresses.

By eight o'clock next morning, the front pews of the church will be filled with little boys bearing palm branches. When the priest comes out to bless the palms, the boys all crowd the communion rail trying to squeeze in for a place nearest the priest. At the Asperges, when the priest sprinkles holy water on the palms, each of the boys will hold his branch as high as possible and shake it in order to catch some of the holy water.

After Mass, everyone goes out to the first *bahay-bahayan* where the little "Angels" are already well settled behind an improvised curtain. At the raising of the curtain, the little girls begin singing the "Hosanna." And as they sing, they throw flowers on the people below. Each little boy tries to catch one flower, so that as a result there is confusion on the ground. After this is over, the

119

people move over to the second platform where the same ceremonial is repeated. At the end of all this, the priest gives his blessing to all present and bids them depart and prepare for Holy Week.

On the way home, the boys proudly distribute some of their blessed palms to older folks waiting by the roadside. And when they arrive home, father and mother will congratulate them for having taken part in such a highly valued custom. As a reward they may receive gifts of toys or new clothes. The blessed palms and the flowers will be carefully stored away by the mother.

Tenebrae

The solemn services of Holy Week begin on Wednesday evening in most Catholic and Protestant churches. The old and dramatic ritual, Tenebrae, used originally in Catholic churches, is now accepted by freer Protestant churches and included in their Wednesday and Thursday night services. The word means "darkness." The candles in the church or sanctuary are extinguished one after the other, until only one candle (representing Christ) remains and is carried behind the altar at the end of the ceremonies.

In Catholic churches the altar is decorated in purple and with six dark yellow candles. To the right of the sanctuary is a triangular wooden frame holding fifteen candles of the same dark color. After each Psalm of Matins and Lauds one of these candles is extinguished, beginning with the bottom one on the gospel side, then the corresponding one on the epistle side, and alternating in that order. The central candle is left burning until toward the end of the service, when it is removed and elevated at the side of the altar, and then hidden behind the altar. After the last prayer has been said, a sign is given with the clapper, and the lighted candle is brought back and placed upon the triangular candlestick. The darkness produced by the gradual extinction of the lights expresses the grief of the Church for the Passion and Death of our Lord, but the reappearance of the lighted candle signifies that His Light was not extinguished with death.

Protestant churches have a beautiful communion service, combining it with the Tenebrae ritual. A table is prepared for Holy Communion, and an additional table is added to form the letter T. In the center of the altar is placed a single conspicuous candle which is lighted. Along two sides of the lower table, which forms the base of the letter T, are eight chairs for the deacons. At each place are a small lighted candle and a card containing certain scriptural passages which are to be read. After the communion service is over, the deacons take their assigned places at the tables and begin to read from the scripture cards the story of the events of that ancient historic night. As each deacon finishes his reading he extinguishes his candle. Synchronizing with the extinguishing of the candles is the slow dimming of the lights of the church. As the last lesson is read the church is in darkness except for the single candle in the center of the altar. Finally that is put out by the minister. Soon the minister relights the center candle, and lights of the church are turned on as symbolic that Easter is soon to dawn.

Holy Thursday

Holy Thursday commemorates our Lord's Last Supper with His disciples. It was on Thursday evening that Jesus celebrated the Passover feast in the upper room of a Jewish friend's home. He used the occasion to fix upon the minds of his disciples a pattern of a memorial service which, later, they were to perform in memory of Him. When He broke bread and meat, He said, "This is my body," then, taking a cup of wine, He said, "This is my blood of the new covenant which is shed for you and for many for the remission of sins." After supper, He discussed at length concerning the Kingdom of God. He also used the occasion for another symbolic gesture—he girded Himself with a towel and washed the feet of the disciples to illustrate the ministry of service.

Ceremony of Washing of Feet. This ancient ceremony is still practiced in some Roman Catholic churches. It symbolizes the commandment of Christ that we should imitate his loving humility in the washing of feet. Originally, it was performed by religious superiors in washing the feet of those subject to them. In medieval times kings and lords washed the feet of the poor men

121

to whom they afterward served a meal and distributed alms.

The ceremony takes on a different interpretation today. In many parishes twelve old men or twelve young boys are chosen. After the Holy Thursday sermon the ceremony takes place in the main sanctuary or right in the body of the church. Chairs are arranged for twelve men (in memory of the twelve Apostles) whose feet will be washed. The deacon leads these men, two by two, to this place while the choir begins singing and the antiphons are said. As many of these as possible are sung or recited while the celebrant washes the right foot of each man in turn.

The Mass of Holy Thursday Evening is one of the most solemn of the year. The priests are dressed in white vestments, the liturgical color of joy, and the cross is covered with a white veil. All the bells in the church are rung and continue to ring until the Gloria is finished. From that moment the bells have a wooden clapper and are not heard again until the Gloria on Saturday morning. In many European countries the silence of the bells is explained to the children by the popular expression "the bells have gone to Rome." A charming old lullaby tells the reason:

The Bells Have Gone to Rome

Do—do—ding, ding dong, sleep little man,
Do—do—ding, ding dong,
The bells have gone to Rome.
It is time to sleep,
The bells have flown away.

They have gone to Rome,
Down there, down there, far away, you see,
To visit the Pope, a saintly man,
An old man dressed in white is he.
The bell of each church
To him secretly speaks
Of all the good little ones,
And he himself, *le Bon Dien* tells
The name of each good little child.

122

Do—do—ding, ding dong, sleep little man.

Stripping of the Altars. After Holy Thursday Mass, a solemn procession takes place in which bishops carry reverently the Blessed Sacrament and place it on the Altar of Repose in the tabernacle, where it remains until Good Friday morning. The altar is richly decorated with candles and flowers and is a highly venerated shrine in every church. It is visited by thousands of people, and in some cities it is a popular custom to visit seven such shrines that day.

When the Mass is ended, the deacon blesses the Holy Sacrament three times and covers it with the ends of the humeral veil. The deacon and sacred ministers then return to the altar, make a reverence, and proceed to strip the other altars. Each altar is stripped except the one on which the Blessed Sacrament is being solemnly adored. During the ceremony the celebrant repeats the 21st Psalm:

> My God, My God, why have You forsaken Me,
>> Far from My prayer, from the words of My cry?
> O My God, I cry out by day . . .

Good Friday

On Good Friday the Passion of our Lord is commemorated as related in the Gospel of Saint John (John 18:1–40). In Catholic churches the altars are completely unadorned, without cross, without linen, without veils. All the statuary is covered with mourning cloth. The impressive ceremony of the day is:

Adoration of the Holy Cross. The celebrating priests unveil the crucifix in three stages singing "Behold the Wood of the Cross on which hung the salvation of the world," to which all answer:

Ve- ní- te,   ad- o-ré- mus.

Then the crucifix is placed on a pillow in front of the altar. The priests and assistants approach it and devotedly kiss the feet of the image. The rest of the lay people follow, performing the same humble act of veneration.

Ceremony of Platsenitsis (Winding Sheet). The Greek Catholics consider Good Friday as one of their most important holy days. On the afternoon of this day, the elders of the parish carry a cloth on which a picture of our Lord's body resting in death is painted or embroidered. Followed by the priest, they walk in procession to the shrine of the Sepulcher, where the cloth is placed on a table to be venerated by the people. Afterward, the priest takes the cloth and carries it around the church placing it inside a carved wooden canopy symbolizing the Tomb of Christ.

Tre Ore Service. Tre Ore (Three Hours) is a well-known Good Friday service of devotion beginning at noon and continuing until three in the afternoon. It was first performed in Lima, Peru, by Father Alphonho Messia and quickly spread to other parts of the world. In America the service is commonly used by both Protestant and Catholic churches. The three-hour devotion is usually built around the last Seven Words of the Cross. At other times the three-hour period is divided into units of one hour each, each one of which is used to present a complete service of worship in the development of some threefold theme. Often one of the Passion oratorios is sung, such as Stainer's "Crucifixion" or Buck's "Story of the Cross." Oratorios on the Seven Words of Christ are also a favorite theme.

Stations of the Cross. The devotion known as the Way of the Cross or the Stations of the Cross first came into use in Western Christendom in the fifteenth century. Its origin is generally sought in the time of the Crusades, when pilgrims to the Holy Land marked off the sites associated with our Lord's Passion in Jerusalem and its environs. On returning to their homes in Europe, they continued their devotion by erecting in their churches, or in the fields, memorials of these stations. All Catholic churches have on their walls pictures or carvings of each scene, and they are also

124

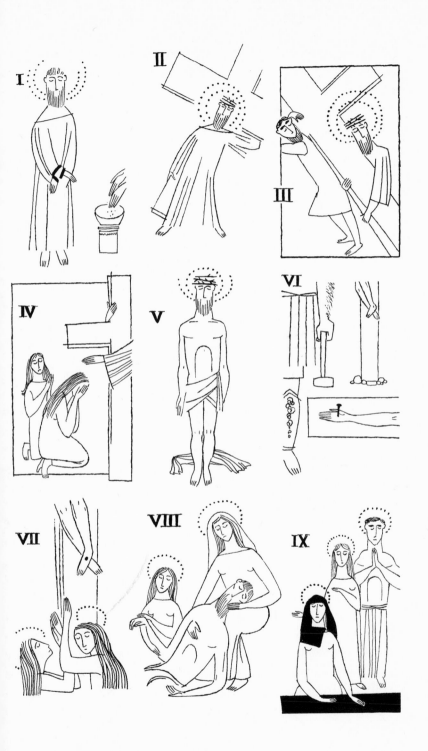

to be found in some Episcopal churches.

The number of stations, no less than the scenes and occasions of the Passion story, varied a great deal. They were fixed at fourteen in the eighteenth century, but five of them have no basis in the Gospel accounts of the Passion. The order of the Stations are as follows:

I—Jesus is condemned to death.
II—Jesus is made to bear His Cross.
III—Jesus falls the first time under His Cross.
IV—Jesus meets His afflicted Mother.
V—Simon helps Jesus to carry His Cross.
VI—Veronica wipes the face of Jesus.
VII—Jesus falls the second time.
VIII—Jesus speaks to the women of Jerusalem.
IX—Jesus falls the third time.
X—Jesus is stripped of His garments.
XI—Jesus is nailed to the Cross.
XII—Jesus dies on the Cross.
XIII—Jesus is taken down from the Cross.
XIV—Jesus is placed in the Sepulcher.

The content of these devotions to the Stations of the Cross has never been determined by any official church authority, for they generally have been considered acts of private prayer and meditation. They have often been observed, however, by groups of worshipers, united in common prayers at each station and in the singing of hymns (usually the *Stabat Mater*) as they passed from one station to another.

Holy Saturday

Saturday of Holy Week is a strange interlude in the Easter festival. It commemorates the day Christ rested in the tomb, the only day of his ministry that he was not alive and present with his friends. The mood is quiet in all cities and towns in somber expectancy, which will turn into radiant joy at the first sight of the evening stars. The faithful keep lights burning all night so their rays will link with the morning sun.

Catholic churches hold a Saturday night service leading directly into Easter morning. Vespers begin with two dramatic rituals.

Blessing of the Easter Fire

The blessing may take place outside the church doors, just within them, or inside the church. Fire is struck from flint in the churchyard, and from it the new Easter fire is lighted. All candles and sanctuary lights are extinguished, to take their light later on from the new fire. A triple taper, representing the Holy Trinity, is lighted and is elevated to lead the procession into the sanctuary where all lights have been extinguished. Then follow the blessing and lighting of the Paschal candle.

The Paschal Candle

The candle symbolizes the body of Jesus and the return of light to the world in the resurrection of Jesus Christ. A priest cuts a cross in wax of the huge candle with a knife. At the top of the cross he cuts the Greek letter alpha and beneath it the Greek letter omega. In the four angles of the cross he writes the four numbers of the coming year, as in the figure below:

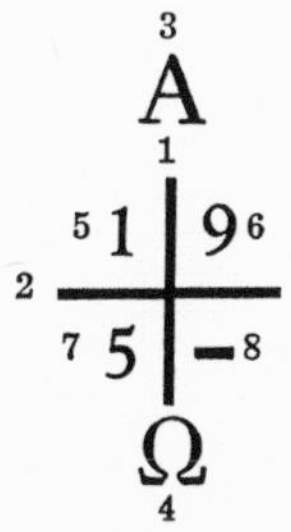

$$\begin{matrix} & 3 & \\ & A & \\ & 1 & \\ ^5 1 & | & 9^6 \\ 2\!\!-\!\!\!&\!\!+\!\!&\!\!\!-\!\! \\ ^7 5 & | & -8 \\ & \Omega & \\ & 4 & \end{matrix}$$

As the cutting is taking place, the priest intones:

1. Christ yesterday and today (he cuts the vertical beam of the cross),

127

2. The Beginning and the End (he cuts the horizontal beam),
3. The Alpha (he cuts the letter A over the vertical beam),
4. And the Omega (he cuts the letter Ω beneath the vertical beam),
5. His are the times (he cuts the first number of the current year in the upper left angle of the cross),
6. And the ages (he cuts the second number of the current year in the upper right angle of the cross),
7. His are the glory and power (he cuts the third number of the current year in the lower left angle of the cross),
8. For all the ages of eternity. Amen (he cuts the fourth number of the current year in the lower right angle of the cross).

The deacon then inserts five grains of incense into the candle in positions indicated in the figure below. They signify the aromatic spices brought by women to anoint the Lord's body. Once they have been fixed, they denote the five wounds of Christ.

1

4   2   5

3

When the candle has been prepared, a deacon hands the priest a small candle that has been lit from the new fire. With it he lights the Paschal Candle, lifts it up, and sings Lumen Christe (Light of Christ). At these words all in the church kneel and answer:

De- o grá-ti-as.   (Thanks be to God.)

Easter Mass

The Solemn Mass of Easter begins with the chanting of the Kyrie:

Lord, have mercy on us. Lord, have mercy on us. Lord, have mercy on us.

Christ, have mercy on us. Christ, have mercy on us. Christ, have mercy on us.

Lord, have mercy on us. Lord, have mercy on us. Lord, have mercy on us.

When the choir completes the Kyrie, the priest solemnly intones the Gloria, the bells begin to ring, and the images are unveiled. Then comes the dramatic moment when the celebrant begins the Alleluia. He sings it three times, raising his voice a little each time. All repeat it each time in the tone the celebrant used:

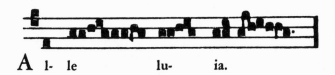

A l- le   lu-   ia.

Greek Church Easter Vigil

The Solemn Easter Vigil in the Greek Church takes on a dramatic scene at midnight. The priest and all the congregation, with lighted candles in their hands, leave the church. The procession walks around to the front door which has been closed (representing the sealed tomb of Christ). The priest slowly makes the sign of the cross with the crucifix he holds in his right hand. At this moment the doors swing open and the people intone the hymn "Christ Is Risen," all the church bells start pealing, and the jubilant procession moves into the brightly illuminated church. The candles in the hands of the worshipers fill the building with a sea of sparkling light.

Protestant Celebrations

Protestant churches conduct Easter Vespers, but with no special rituals. A good many Episcopal churches schedule the first Vespers of Easter and the lighting of the Paschal Candle as an afternoon service for Holy Saturday. One service which is an adaptation of this ancient candle ceremony is used in other churches. It begins with the prophecies of the Messiah read in the nave by the minister, and the triple cluster of candles is lighted and held aloft. The minister and choir lead a processional to the chancel where the choir takes its place in the stalls. A cluster of lights is placed in candle holders on the altar, and the Passion lesson is read by the minister. During the reading, deacons proceed to light all the candles in the church, and at the same time the altar is adorned with festive coverings.

JOYOUS EASTER

Easter, a festival rooted deep in the human heart, is one Sunday in the year when all Christians attend the church of their choice. Not even Christmas, unless it happens to fall on a Sunday, can match Easter for church-going. America is the happy inheritor of faiths and customs of other lands, and the music of church bells brings amity and drowns prejudice. To all, Easter has one meaning: Death is foiled of victory; life steps forth from the grave renewed and triumphant.

On this day America unites with all the world and with all ages. Protestant churches now vie with Roman Catholic in services of richness and splendor. Often the religious feeling overflows from the churches to the outdoors and to special observations throughout the country. All this makes the Easter festival the greatest Christian celebration of the year because, after all, before there was a Christmas, there were Easters.

PAGEANTRY OF EASTER

At Easter, a sage has said, we "dramatize man's divinity in the midst of his mortality." Most impressive, perhaps, is the custom

f going to the hilltop to watch for Easter dawn. Multitudes gather
n the darkness, and amid a hush of meditation and expectation
urn their eyes toward the western sky. When the notes are those
f Handel's immortal air, "I Know That My Redeemer Liveth,"
he mystic spell is complete. There is new contact between man
nd the universe, and the beautiful custom has captured the land:

Sunrise Services

At New England colleges—Mount Holyoke, among others—the
tudents come together on mountaintops, in parks, and on shores
f lakes to welcome the morning sunrise. On the West Coast a
rowd of 50,000 can be expected in the Hollywood Bowl at sun-
ise, one of 30,000 in a Los Angeles park, and a pilgrimage of
0,000 to greet the day on the slopes of Mount Rubidoux. When
laster morn dawns in San Francisco, thousands will be on the
ugged sides of Mount Davidson, on whose summit gleams a great
ghted cross.

Near Colorado Springs is held one of the most picturesque of
unrise services. The setting is that beautiful natural temple, the
arden of the Gods, with its pulpit rock, its pillars and needle
pires of red stone, and Pike's Peak looking down from overhead.
rom western states for miles around come people by the thou-
ands to share in the stirring moment when the sunlight flashes
cross the plain and invisible musicians fill the cathedral with
eals of joyful sound.

God's Acre

The Moravians in this country cling to Old World habits and
dd a glowing bit of color to the American Easter picture. Their
orship begins on Palm Sunday and continues through Passion
Veek, as it has done in their ancestral land since John Huss and
he Reformation. Crowds of pious folk and sightseers swarm to
ethlehem, in Pennsylvania, and to the historic little brick church
Winston-Salem, North Carolina, to witness the Easter festival.
he events of the life of the Lord are dramatized day by day

131

during Holy Week, and the ceremony called "God's Acre" takes place in the early hours Easter morning.

In the darkness of the early morning church members gather to make their way by light of torches up the hillside to God's Acre. As they stand among the simply marked graves, singing their songs of hope and faith, watching the rising sun drive darkness from hills and valleys, there comes a deeper appreciation of the Resurrection truth.

Today a great company of musicians is needed in the service. Drawn from churches and chapels that compose all the Moravian churches, they are carefully trained to render with perfection the beautiful antiphonal chorales and hymns that so greatly enhance the service.

It offers to those who attend in the spirit of true worship an opportunity much needed in our busy modern world and gives expression to a truth: "The Lord is risen!"

Because He is risen and now reigns, the dead whose mortal remains sleep in so many God's Acres—"Those of our brethren and sisters who since last Easter day have entered into the joy of our Lord"—also live.

The early Easter service closes with a burst of triumphant music from the horns, music that says to those familiar words—

> Sing hallelujah, praise the Lord,
>   Sing with a cheerful voice,
> Exalt our God with one accord
>   And His name rejoice,
> Ne'er cease to sing, thou ransomed host,
>   Praise Father, Son and Holy Ghost,
> Until in realms of endless light
>   Your praises shall unite.

Easter Parades

The Easter Parade which is held after church services in many cities is another survival from long ago. Before there were couturiers or fashion pages there was a lively superstition, dear to

132

princesses and peasant maidens alike, that a new garment worn at Easter meant good luck throughout the year. The glad raiments also reflect the broader ancient idea that Easter is the time of newness and a fresh start. This brightest contribution to the Easter festival has declined a bit in recent years, but the crowds still dress in their best to make a colorful show at Easter.

The Easter Rabbit

The white rabbit of Easter, beloved of small Americans, comes hopping down to us from eras when the sun and the moon were gods to men. The pure white rabbit played in the full of the pure white Easter moon and brought gifts of bright colored eggs to children who were good. Some religious authorities would like to outlaw eggs and rabbits along with Santa Claus—"These things paganize religion," we are told. But eggs and rabbits please the youngsters today just as white sweet lilies gladden the old.

Egg Rolling

The Easter Monday Egg Rolling on the White House lawn asks no ecclesiastical sanction; it has become a national institution, to be mentioned in the same breath as the Fourth of July. In this unique affair 50,000 people take part or look on. The children take possession of the south lawn—fountains and pools must be protected with netting, and a lost and found department organized. The children roll the eggs in streams down the green terraces, and then recover their basketful and roll them again, and in their exuberance they themselves roll down. There is no other custom quite like it in the world!

Lenten Foods

The tradition of the Paschal lamb perhaps inspired the use of lamb meat as a popular food at Eastertime. Frequently, however, little figures of a lamb made of butter, pastry, or sugar have been substituted for the meat, forming Easter table centerpieces. Spiced meat of some kind is a popular Easter dish; and, of course, there is the custom of eating as many eggs as possible for breakfast.

133

Lenten foods are most interesting, and there are enough recipes to fill a good-size cookbook, but we would like to mention three because of their historical background:

Hot-Cross Buns. Many of our Easter customs have existed since time immemorial, and continue today, dressed in new meanings. The hot-cross bun, for example, is pagan in origin. The Anglo-Saxon savages consumed cakes as a part of the jollity that attended the welcoming of spring. The early missionaries from Rome despaired of breaking them of the habit, and got around the difficulty at last by blessing the cakes, drawing a cross upon them. Come Ash Wednesday hot-cross buns appear in every bakery window and, interestingly enough, are only sold during the Easter season.

Pretzels. Christians in the Roman Empire made a special dough consisting of flour, salt, and water only, since fat, eggs, and milk were forbidden. They shaped it into the form of two arms crossed in prayer to remind them that Lent was a season of penance and devotion. They called these breads *Bracalle* (Little Arms). From the Latin word, the Germans later coined the term brezel or prezel, from which comes our word pretzel. In many parts of Europe pretzels remain a Lenten food. They make their annual appearance on Ash Wednesday, and special vendors sell them on the streets of villages and towns; then they disappear until the following Ash Wednesday.

134

Fromajadas. Before the middle of the last century an ancient and pleasing Minorcan custom was brought to St. Augustine by settlers. On Easter Eve, bands of young men went about the streets singing, beneath the windows, to the accompaniment of guitar and violin, their hymn of praise to the Virgin (translated):

> Ended the days of sadness
> Grief gives way to singing
> We come with joy and gladness
> Our gifts to Mary bring.

Approaching the dwelling of someone whom they wished to favor with their song, or from whom they might expect the favors asked in their rhyme, they would knock gently upon the window or tap on the shutter. If their visit was welcome they were answered by a knock from within and would at once begin the song in their dialect. If no reply was heard, they would pass to another house. After the hymn, a verse soliciting the customary gifts or eggs was sung:

> The owner of this house
> Ought to give us a token.
> Either a cake or a tart
> We like anything
> So you say not no.

If they sang well, the shutters were then opened and a supply of cakes or other pastry was dropped into a bag carried by one of the party, who acknowledged the gift by proclaiming:

> The owner of this house
> Is a polite gentleman.

Or, if no gifts were forthcoming, the last line went

> The owner of this house
> Is not a polite gentleman.

The song was repeated throughout the city until midnight. The favorite cake was made of cheese, hence the song was called

Fromajadas, or the cheesecake song. From a book of *Spanish and Minorcan Recipes* by Mrs. Katherine S. Lawson and Mrs. Mary Lee Gannon comes this recipe for Fromajadas cakes:

"Much variety exists in making the pastry." The usual method calls for "rich pastry," made with lard or butter or any standard shortening. A small amount of baking powder may or may not be used. Most directions call for some "lightening." Your favorite pie dough will suffice. Now—

Roll the dough thin. Cut in rounds about the size of a saucer, or smaller. Cut a cross on one half of each round. Grate one pound of cheese. Beat six eggs and beat into the cheese. Flavor with either or both, cinnamon or nutmeg. Add a little hot pepper. Place a spoonful of this mixture on unslashed half of round dough. Turn slash-half over the cheese and pinch edges together. Bake in medium oven until pale brown. *The filling puffs up through the cross.*

Symbols of Easter Day

Cross. It signifies that Christ died for mankind. There are many styles of crosses, as shown on page 36, each with its own symbol.

Ass. This Castilian donkey has a dark patch of hair which goes the length of his back, and another which crosses his shoulder. Since this is the animal Christ chose to ride when he made his triumphal entry into Jerusalem, the legends . . . say, the ass will always bear the cross.

Owl. It strangely prefers darkness to light. Traditionally it is a symbol of people always in darkness.

Robin. They say a robin plucked a thorn from the forehead of Christ, staining its breast red. Since then all robins are red-breasted.

Lion. Ancient people believe that lion cubs were born dead and that when they were three days old the lioness breathed on them and brought them to life, signifying that Christ lay dead three days in the Tomb and then lived again.

Whales. Many people thought the story of Jonah was a proph-

136

ecy. It told that for three days Jonah lay in the belly of a great fish and then was cast up on dry land. Just so, Jesus came forth again into light of the world.

Phoenix. It is believed the phoenix lived for 300–500 years. Every so often this mythical bird would cast itself on a funeral pyre and be consumed in flames. Then it would arise from its own ashes and begin life all over again. It was thought this signified that one can die and be born again.

Butterfly. Its whole life is symbolic of the meaning of Christianity. First, the caterpillar which stands for life, then the cocoon which signifies death, and finally the butterfly which emerges portraying the Resurrection.

Rabbit. It is said to be frail and dependent on the goodness of others, representing man, who placed his hope in Christ.

Eagle. It was thought the eagle restored its life after flying so close to the sun its feathers were scorched and burned. It is also the only bird that can look directly at the light of the sun.

Swallow. On the day Christ was crucified, the little bird called to him, "Cheer up! Cheer up!" From that time the bird became known as the bird of consolation, or swallow.

5. PENTECOST CYCLE

In this cycle two deity festivals are celebrated—Pentecost and Holy Trinity. Today both festivals are merely celebrated in church liturgy on designated Sundays, but in early centuries, they assumed great importance in the year's celebrations. They were the heralds of spring and came during the season of the Jewish Feast of Weeks. In England the festival was called "May Day" and in Scandinavian countries "St. John's Day." Other celebrations in the Pentecost Cycle have to do with secular holidays such as Memorial Day, All Saints' Day, and Thanksgiving. In between are civic holidays and special church days that are recognized with appropriate church services.

PENTECOST

The date of Pentecost is always dependent upon the date of Easter, for it comes seven weeks after the Festival of the Resurrection. It was on this day that the Apostles were gathered in the upper room in Jerusalem to celebrate the Jewish festival, Feast of Weeks. Above them appeared parted tongues as if of fire, which settled upon each of them, and they were all filled with the Holy Spirit and began to speak in foreign tongues. Thus was fulfilled the promise that Christ made at the Last Supper that

138

"though He must leave them, He would abide in them and send the Holy Spirit to comfort them and teach them all truth." The Apostles were transformed from timid and fearful men into courageous and dynamic ministers who were able to go and evangelize the world. Thus the church was fully established and set upon the mission of salvation.

In Catholic churches no special liturgical ceremonies take place aside from the Saturday Vigil. Mass on Pentecost Sunday is celebrated in symbolic vestments of red and is a glorious drama when enacted by the clergy among decorations and a specially arranged chant.

In the Episcopal and free Protestant churches, Pentecost Sundays are used for confirmation of faith and baptism of new members. All Christian churches celebrate Holy Communion on this day.

The dove is used to symbolize Pentecost in all forms of art and in many churches. It is the custom to have a painted dove suspended over the altar during Mass, and some families hang one over their dining table.

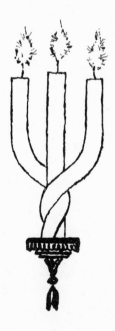

The Sunday after Pentecost is known as the Festival of the Holy Trinity. The doctrine of the Holy Trinity often confuses not only the ordinary layman but also theologians. It is enough for Christians to know that the doctrine is merely an attempt on the part of man to set forth the infinite mystery and the Divine Being. The nature of the Trinity, therefore, must always be set forth in a symbolic way.

The making of the sign of the cross, which professes faith in both the redemption of Christ and the Trinity, was practiced from earliest centuries. The ancient Christian doxology (prayer of praise)—"Glory be to the Father, and to the Son, and to the Holy Ghost"—is used in most Christian churches.

Many imaginative symbolic pictures as well as designs are used to indicate the great mystery of the Trinity. Best known is the shamrock used by Saint Patrick to illustrate the truth to his followers. A second plant to which this symbolism is attached is the pansy (*Viola tricolor*), which is sometimes called trinity flower.

On Trinity Sunday churches display three tapers joined together at the base to symbolize the day. Many churches bear architectural numbers of three in honor of the Trinity, such as three animals or three interlocked circles. The most remarkable example of this kind is found in the Trinity Church of Stasl-Paura, Austria, built in 1722. It has three aisles, three towers, three bells, three doors, three windows on either side, three altars, and three rows of pews.

OTHER RELIGIOUS CELEBRATIONS

Corpus Christi

In the thirteenth century in a convent near Liége, a young nun, called Juliana of Retinnes (Retinnes being the town of her birth), had a vision of the moon in splendor but with part of the sphere broken away. Imploring God's help to understand its meaning, it was revealed to her that the moon represented the Church, but the break indicated the lack of a solemnity in honor of the Eucha-

rist. Three years later, the Pope directed that a celebration in the form of a festival take place in honor the Blessed Sacrament to be held the Thursday after Trinity Sunday.

Very early the custom developed of carrying the Blessed Sacrament in a splendid procession through the town after Mass on Corpus Christi Sunday. In Catholic countries the procession developed into a splendid pageant of grandeur and devotion. It was led by clerics dressed in white and gold vestments followed by sovereigns and princes, presidents and members of state, magistrates, members of trade guilds, honor guards of the armed forces, all carrying their own banners, which created a splendid spectacle indeed.

It is only in Europe, in Spain, Italy, France, and Portugal, that the grandeur of the procession is still carried on. In many villages the Sacrament is carried over a thick bed of rose petals, and houses take on gay decorations. Crucifixes and pictures of Christ are prominently displayed from window ledges, steps of cottages, and fountains. In many places people display bright hangings and spread carpets before their houses in honor of the Sacrament. At Genzano, Spain, the flowers are arranged in great squares and woven into intricate designs so as to form huge pictures, like mosaics. Noted artists are hired to make plans for the panels, and skilled workmen produce the scenes.

In America the grandeur of the procession is dispensed with except in villages along the Mexican border, but the liturgy is the same everywhere. At the end of the Mass, the celebrant is vested in a cope and a veil is put around his shoulders; with the ends of this he grasps a gold or silver vessel for holding the circular

141

crystal in which the Blessed Sacrament is exposed and faces the people. A procession is formed behind the white standard of the Eucharist, and as the people fall in line, they sing hymns from the office of the day. Whether the procession takes place outside or within the church, everyone returns to the main altar for the benediction.

In Texas, cities and towns bordering on Mexico that have a large Latin population still adhere to the outdoor celebration. One of the picturesque aspects of the festival is the *reposiar*, or small altars which the villagers set up along highways, particularly at crossroads. These shrines are covered with hand-embroidered or lace-trimmed altar cloths and decorated with candles, flowers, and garlands of greens. Canopies of interwoven green branches give the altars the appearance of woodland chapels. The priest gives his benediction to these places of worship as he makes his village rounds.

A quaint custom of having a "mock market" set up along the path of the procession is for the benefit of the children. Each occupation manufactures miniature objects of his trade and displays them in various stalls; builders make doll houses, restaurant keepers set up small tables and serve small portions in miniature dishes, weavers offer tiny blankets and belts for sale, and farmers exhibit seeds of what they grow. Bakers make inch-size bread which the children use for money, and when they ask "How much?" a reduction in price is given!

Mother's Day

On May 9, 1914, President Woodrow Wilson issued a proclamation directing officials to display the national flag on all government buildings, and asking people also to hang out their flags on the second Sunday in May as "a public expression of our love and reverence for mothers in our country." In recommending such a holiday to the Congress, the President spoke of the home as "the fountainhead of the State" and of mothers as being influential in good government and humanity. It is customary for children to wear a pink carnation on this day in honor of a living

142

mother and a white if the mother has passed away. The choice of a carnation was made in memory of President William McKinley, who had always worn a white carnation because it was his mother's favorite flower.

The counterpart of Mother's Day is Father's day which falls on the third Sunday in June. President Calvin Coolidge recommended the national observance of the day in 1924. The rose is the official Father's Day flower. A white rose for remembrance, and a red rose as a tribute to a living father.

The Commission on Worship of the Federal Council of Churches of Christ has suggested a change from Mother's Day to the Festival of the Christian Home. An increasing number of Protestant churches are now using the second Sunday in May with emphasis on the family rather than motherhood. Sermons are preached which attempt to help the various members of American households to develop patterns of action that will inspire them to live normal and responsible lives.

Children's Day

Like many American customs, Children's Day has its roots in the Old World. In most European countries the Roman Catholics and Lutherans set aside one day a year for confirmation and baptism of children; in England it was on May Day. The Reverend Charles H. Leonard, pastor of the Universalist Church of the Redeemer, Chelsea, Massachusetts, designated a special day for the baptism of children in his congregation. This was in 1856 and he named it "Rose Day." This probably explains the baptismal ceremony many pastors use today of dipping a rose into water and sprinkling it over the child's forehead.

It was the Methodist Episcopal Church that was the first to proclaim formally a Children's Day in 1868. It falls on the second Sunday in June and is observed in most Protestant Sunday Schools. In small churches the children usually march down the aisle of the church and fill the front pews, but in large city churches, the service is limited to the various Sunday School departments. The more ambitious Church Schools might present a playette or a

143

series of tableaux of Bible stories. There is no set program.

The church service is usually given over to parents, who are urged to bring their children to be baptized on this day.

Rally Day

Rally Day is the day that marks the official opening of the new year in Protestant churches. The Sunday designated for the celebration is optional with individual churches, but it is usually in the last part of September or the first week in October. By this time planning committees have programs set for fall and winter, and people are home from vacations.

The observance of Rally Day varies greatly with each local parish. It usually begins by having all Sunday School departments meet together in the nave of the church. This is an unusually interesting experience for the children because during the rest of the year they meet in their separate departments. Sometimes the program is a promotion exercise where children are graduated from one department to another. When churches can afford it, a child is presented with his first Bible.

The idea of Rally Day may be carried through into the church service. The minister may use the occasion for welcoming new members, or he may underline the basic purposes and activities of the church for the coming year.

6. RELIGIOUS DRAMA

The history of every civilization reveals that its drama has grown out of its early religious ceremonies. Today we have come to see what makes a play religious; it is not the material it deals with but the total effect of the play on the audience. If a play sends an audience away exalted in spirit and with a deep sense of fellowship with God and man, it has been religious.

Churches all over America have drama groups. It is an absorbing way to spend an evening either watching or participating in a play. Nearly every individual belongs to a society of some sort which may be for dancing, singing, art, lighting, etc., the skills that are needed to put on a drama production. It offers an excuse for men and women to be together and an excellent activity for teen-agers as well as children. Churches looking for ways to integrate a congregation can find no better offering than a play of some kind.

Most modern churches begin with pageantry, presenting certain ideas in the form of living pictures accompanied with music. Dramatizing Bible stories helps the Sunday School to rediscover experiences of old Biblical characters and interpret their influence on religion today. Plays devoted to missionary work open up opportunities for deeds of heroism, and traditions and customs of other lands might be included.

145

From earliest days drama has played an important role in the function of the church. For one thing, the people could not read the Bible, so the first plays were presented by the clerics themselves. These were played inside the church by ecclesiastics, but later, during the latter half of the nineteenth century, laymen began performing them in different parts of the city or town. Plays and sometimes a series of plays were produced on a platform set up in the churchyard or village green. The platforms were simple wooded structures that could be moved from place to place, or sometimes they were carried in processions and set up at different stations along the line of march.

We wish we had space to describe the various forms drama has taken down through the ages, but anyone interested can find numerous books on the subject in their local library. Old customs, like using statues of holy figures for characters in a play, the use of marionettes and puppets, Passion plays where the actors live in character throughout the year, make fascinating reading and give inspiration to a dramatic group to plan a simple religious play.

Here is a brief description of outstanding characteristics of some early dramatic forms that can easily be applied to religious productions today.

Theatre in the Round

The theatre in the round originated in England during the Reformation when plays or public gatherings were forbidden by the government. It became the vogue of gentry to hire professional actors and to produce plays in great ballrooms of their own castle. The production took place in the center of the room with the audience seated on all four sides. The lords and ladies and dignitaries were ranged in front rows according to class. Often they were invited by the actors to "step on stage" and perform a special skill.

This form is widely used today for musical productions in summer theatres. It means very simply the proscenium stage is disposed of and the actors are placed in a lighted arena surrounded

on all four sides by spectators. The few props are carried on and off stage as episodes and acts are changed.

Masked Play or Masked Pantomime

The stage for a masked play usually has a backdrop of a blue sky. From time to time birds or clouds made of paper pass in front of it. Rabbits or other animals, the size of a child's toy, scurry in and around the feet of the actors.

The masks fit entirely over heads of the actors, and because there are no openings, they show their feelings by body movements and hand gestures. In other words, interpretive dancing and rhythmic actions substitute for actual speech.

Any dialogue is sung or spoken by a set of side singers who sit with accompanying instruments. At the beginning, they sing out each character's name so the audience can recognize him as he moves about.

Asian Drama Form

Asian drama is built on certain broad principles stemming from India's past that make it different from drama found in other parts of the world. Broadly speaking, the three root elements are simple poetry, music, and dance. This type of production requires two main characters:

A *storyteller*, who acts the role of "reciter." He sings or declaims the most important poetic passages.

147

A *string holder,* who introduces the numbers and fills in important facts that are needed for the interpretation.

On the side are what might be called narrators. They form a special group who add extra gestures to what is being said, play simple instruments, or chant, as the production requires.

Since the drama is primarily the acting of poetry, time and place are not important. The actor, therefore, is not required to set his scene or spread a backdrop.

Mime

Mime is an ancient art that knows no language barrier because there is no spoken word. The mime's trick is to make us see what is not there and feel what is happening without the actual causations being present. It is an art that includes clowning, ballet, acrobatics, and acting; the show can be funny or sad.

Today mime, or pantomime, is most popularly used in creative dance forms based on folk materials. Dvora Lapson, whose dances are reproduced in this book, is an internationally recognized mime dancer. The Bible assumes a richer meaning when her sketches of Ruth, David, Elijah, and Esther take form. In her books, she has worked themes of Jewish life and customs into folk dances, such as the quaint Sabbath Ceremonial with the blessing of the candles and the welcoming of the Queen Sabbath into the home.

Folk dancers who mime religious ceremonials or some of the beautiful harvest customs create a positive emotional response, not only from the audience but also among themselves. For example, Mrs. Mimi Boaz Kingsley and her group of Mexican dancers presented a pantomime of the Mexican Christmas celebration, a mimed scene in which Joseph and Mary are invited into the inn. When the group as a whole participated in this symbolic dance, they found their own emotions more completely involved than if they had participated merely in a folk dance as such.

Mystery Plays

Mystery plays, sometimes called morality plays dealt respectively with Biblical stories, legends of saints, and subjects which

148

illustrated moral truths. They were produced outdoors on crude wooden platforms that could be moved from place to place. Here a whole cycle of plays, anywhere from fifteen to fifty, were performed in sequence. The creation of the world was one of the most popular subjects, with Noah's ark running a close second.

One of the interesting things about the early mystery plays was that licenses to run them were issued to craftsmen's guilds. For instance, cooks presented the harrowing Hell Scenes because they were used to baking and broiling things, and knew how to take them out and put them back into an oven. Watermen prepared the Noah's ark play, and shiprights supervised the construction of the ark. The fishmongers completed the production adding water for the flood!

In America every year, during January and sometimes on into February, a mystery play takes place very much the same as it might have been produced three hundred years ago. A description of it may give a better idea of how effective one can be.

The Shepherds

In San Antonio, Corpus Christi, the Rio Grande, and other Latin parts of Texas, Christmas brings the sounds of guitars, and along the streets are men selling herbs, red peppers, and paper flowered decorated altars of the Nativity. Against this background the strange and highly colored *Los Pastores* (The Shepherds), a medieval drama, is to be given with modern insertions.

This drama came to these Spanish-Americans with the *padres*, and the lines have been passed down from generation to generation, so the play is given without script. It is presented nightly as long as the people want it and the admission is free.

Originally, the play was given in the churches, but now the drama is presented in the backyard with a stage that holds only a few "props." On one side stands a table with a statue of Joseph and Mary and the baby Jesus. On the other is a canvas booth with a monstrous painted face—Hell, from which evil beings will emerge.

There are twenty-four characters in the play, and all of them

149

have long roles and a great deal to say. First, comes the Angel Gabriel to tell the shepherds that Christ has been born. There are fourteen herdsmen dressed in pastoral costumes. With the shepherds is the *Hermitano,* or Hermit, dressed in a Franciscan habit with cowl and beads, and a lazy comic called Bartolo, who sleeps as often as he can and rests if he does not sleep. When he is awakened with word that the Savior has been born, he yawns and suggests they carry him along on a mattress.

The shepherds start on their way to Bethlehem, when they suddenly realize they have had no supper. Thereupon, logically, they eat a good meal, which is provided by the owner of the house in whose yard the drama takes place. That over, they go back to the play. But, now, there is a disturbance—all kinds of devils spring out of Hell to attack the shepherds. Children scream and women cover their faces at the horrid figures. The main devil and his assistants are dressed in black with red caps; some have horns made of antlers, and others carry sparklers. They talk in sepulchral tones and begin to thwart the shepherds and tempt them by appealing to their all-too-human instincts.

A long battle between good and evil ensues. The audience takes an eager part in every moment of the play. When the shepherds suffer, it groans; when they triumph, it exalts. Finally, toward the end, the main devil encounters St. Michael, the little boy, who, even though he is much smaller and weaker, is the victor in battle.

The play ends when the shepherds reach the table on which rests the Holy Family. They bow in adoration and place their gifts before the Christ Child. The conclusion is particularly touching when the shepherds take leave of the manger and sing their farewell:

> Good-by Joseph, Good-by Mary
> Good-by, my very little Baby . . .
> Give us life and health to return another year.

7. BIBLICAL GARDENS

The Bible is rich in its allusion to flowers, spices, and herbs. In the Songs of Solomon, flowers run across the pages of the eight short chapters—apple blossoms, henna flowers, lilies, banks of sweet herbs, beds of spices, orchards, vineyards, and palm groves. Planting a garden on church property is an excellent project, as many members like to garden and care for plants. The flowers can be used for church decoration or sent to a person who is ill, and herbs are easily processed and dried to be sold at church bazaars. If you want to plant a Biblical garden there are many books on the subject. Here are a few suggestions to get you started:

Herbs from the Holy Land
A General Use for All Manner of Herbs

It is a general rule from the Eight Kalends of the moneth of Aprill until the moneth of July all manner of leaves of hearbes be best and from the Eight Kalends of July until the Eight Kalends of October the stalks have most virtue and from the Eight Kalends of Aprill all manner of roots of hearbes be in their full strength.

17th Century manuscript in British Museum

It is traditional to plant herbs around a sundial or along the banks of gardens. Many herbs flourish best in front of a stone wall. In general, an herb garden should be in a sunny spot with loose sandy soil. We have selected only the common varieties of herbs, but you will find that many exotic ones are found in the lands of the Bible:

Anethum graveolens, the dill. This plant is a common weed in the grainfields of Palestine and is sometimes referred to as "anise." It is cultivated for its seeds, which are aromatic and carminative, and similar to those of caraway. The seeds are used in cookery to flavor dishes, particularly in green salads.

Cuminum cyminum, the cummin. In Isaiah and Matthew we read of cummin. This is an annual plant of the carrot family, native to Egypt and the eastern Mediterranean region. It grows only about six inches tall, but has long been cultivated for its aromatic seeds, which are similar to dill seeds but are larger. In Palestine these seeds are used extensively as a flavoring material and even minced with flour in breadmaking.

Coriandrum sativum, the coriander. The coriander is common as a weed among grain throughout the Holy Land. It was used by the ancients both as a condiment and as a medicine. A favorite drink was made by steeping the whole plant in wine. The seeds, afterward dried and thus rendered milder, were eaten with various dishes. The fragrant leaves are used even today in soups, puddings, curries, and wine. The seeds of cummin and coriander were spread on bread and pastry as poppy seeds are used today.

Crocus sativus, the saffron crocus. In the Song of Solomon we read of saffron. It is the product of several species of crocus, especially the blue-flowered one. It consists of the stigmas and parts of the style, which are gathered when the flower first opens. It requires about four stigmas to make an ounce of saffron, which explains the high cost of the condiment in stores today. After gathering, the stigmas either are dried in the sunshine and pounded or are made into little cakes. Saffron is used principally as a yellow dye or for coloring curries.

Allium sativum, the garlic. Garlic is a hardy bulbous perennial

152

which occurs wild, as well as cultivated, in Europe, western Asia, and Egypt, as it doubtless also did at the time of Moses. It is well known as a culinary stimulant and is very popular with all the peoples inhabiting the Mediterranean region. There are about forty-two different kinds of onion and garlic recorded from the Holy Land area.

Brassica nigra, the black mustard. The "mustard seed" of Jesus' famous parable doubtless came from the black mustard which had the smallest seed with which the farmers of his day were acquainted. Although it is only an annual plant, its stems and branches in autumn become hard and rigid and of quite sufficient strength to bear the weight of birds, which are attracted to it by their seeds.

Hyssophus officinalis, hyssop. Many plants have been called "hyssop," and the hyssop of the Bible is now supposed to have been one of the marjorams. In the Middle Ages hyssop added bitter taste to soup, pickles, meat pies, and poultry seasonings. Saint John wrote in Chapter 19:29, at the Crucifixion: "There was set a vessel full of vinegar; and they filled a sponge with vinegar and put it upon hyssop and put it in His mouth."

The *spikenard* in the Bible is *lavender,* and it was said the Mother of God was very fond of this herb for the reason that is preserves chastity: "If the head is sprinkled with lavender water it will make that person chaste as long as he bears it upon him." In Chapter 4 of Saint Mark, 3, 4, 5, when Christ was in the home of the leper, "There came a woman having an alabaster box of ointment of spikenard, very precious and she broke the box and poured it on His head . . . and there were some that had indignation within themselves and said 'why was this waste of ointment made?' For it might have been sold for more than three hundred talents and given to the poor."

A "Mary" Garden

It was especially upon the Virgin Mary that the wealth of flowers was lavished, so it is not difficult to find any number of plants to make a "Mary Garden." All white flowers were considered

typical of her purity and holiness and are consecrated to her festivals. Of all flowers, the rose is most closely associated with the Virgin Mary because it is said to have first blossomed at Our Savior's birth, closed at the Crucifixion, and opened again at Easter. In art one finds that artists through the ages have used the rose to express their ideals of beauty. In Botticelli's "Coronation of the Virgin," the air is literally filled with roses falling from Heaven, symbols of the love of God.

One of the most picturesque rose miracles is the creation of the rosary, which is found in the early history of almost every Christian country. The story is told and retold of the young man who made the Virgin an offering of 150 roses each day. The roses he wove into a wreath for her altar. Eventually he became a monk in an austere order, and in his new way of life it bothered him that he had neither time nor opportunity to continue performing the devotion to his adored Lady. The Abbe whom he consulted advised him, instead, to say 150 Aves to the Blessed Virgin each day, assuring him that they would be just as acceptable to her as his daily offering of roses. Thereafter at a certain hour each day the young man knelt at the altar of the Blessed Virgin repeating the required number of Aves.

A worthy Franciscan said, "Mindful of the festivals which our church prescribes, I have sought to make these objects of floral nature timepieces of my Religious Calendar: Thus, I can light the taper to our Virgin Mother on the blooming of the White Snowdrop which opens its flowers at the time of Candlemas. The Lady's

154

Smok and Daffodil remind me of the Annunciation, the Blue Bell of the Festival of St. George; Ronunculus of the Invention of the Cross; the Scarlet Lichen of St. John the Baptist, and the White Lily of the Visitation of Our Lady."

Here are a few legendary flowers to plant in a "Mary" Garden:

Rosemary. It is said that the blososms on this plant were originally white. However, they turned blue (Mary's color) in reward for service it offered when Our Lady looked for some bush on which to spread her sky-blue gown on her way from Bethlehem.

Thistle. Our Lady's thistle has green leaves spotted with white caused by some drops of the Virgin's milk flowing upon them.

Lily-of-the-Valley is sometimes called "Our Lady's Tears." It is the favorite flower in many countries to decorate her shrine for the Feast of Annunciation (March 25).

Foxglove, because of its bell-shaped flowers covered with small black dots, is called Our Lady's thimbles.

Snowdrop. This delicate flower blossoms early in the spring, sometimes between patches of melting snow. Little bouquets of snowdrops are the first floral tribute of the year to shrines of the Madonna.

Lily. This stately, dignified flower has been associated with Jesus and Mary since early times. It is used at Easter to symbolize radiance of the Lord's risen life.

Peace Gardens

There has been an increasing interest shown throughout the country in Peace Gardens, memorial rose gardens. The peace rose was born out of agony of crucified France in World War II. In Jacksonville, Florida, a beautiful Peace Memorial Park has been planted with two hundred symbolic peace roses as a tribute to the American fighting men. The project was developed by a Gold Star Mother, when she saw the park of Belgian roses in Quebec, Canada, planted by war widows of World War I.

8. NOTES

The Four Evangelists

It is said that everything has a symbolic meaning. Very often Jesus Christ is represented surrounded by the lion, the eagle, the calf, and the winged man; they represent the four evangelists. The winged man represents St. Matthew, because he began his gospel by giving a genealogy of the ancestors of Christ. The lion represents St. Mark, who began his gospel by speaking of the voice in the desert. The calf is St. Luke, who commenced with the sacrifice offered by Zacharias. The eagle is St. John, who speaks of the Divinity, and like the eagle can look at the sun, the sun being Jesus himself.

Star Symbols

We have always given stars a high place in the realm of symbolism. The various number of points has held different significance to the beholder.

The four-pointed star is called the Cross Étoile, and its very name explains its meaning: the star cross.

The five-pointed star is the Star of Epiphany. It is symbolic of the manifestation of the birth of Jesus to the Gentiles, as it tells us of the journey of the Wise Men to Bethlehem.

The six-pointed star is the Star of David and is used as a decoration on synagogues, denoting that there is a place of worship; on the sacred vessels; etc. The six points are said to refer to the attributes of God: power, wisdom, majesty, love, mercy, and justice.

The seven-pointed star reminds us of the seven gifts of the Holy Ghost: power, wealth, wisdom, might, honor, glory, and blessing.

The eight-pointed star is the star of regeneration, telling us of the seven days of creation plus the era of grace which came after, and also the gift of baptism. The use of the number eight is reflected in octagonal baptismal fonts in use in many churches.

The nine-pointed star indicates the nine fruits of the Holy Ghost: love, joy, peace, long-suffering, gentleness, goodness, faith, mildness, and temperance (Galatians 5:22).

The ten-pointed star reminds us of the ten apostles who neither denied nor betrayed their Lord.

The twelve-pointed star is the symbol for the twelve apostles and also the twelve tribes of Israel.

THE HEAVENLY HOST

In fine old Byzantine churches and in days of Gothic art, it was customary to picture *Nine Choirs of Angels* surrounding the throne of God. The idea of various choirs is supposed to date back to Old Testament days, and Jewish people of old were familiar with the various ranks of heavenly beings.

The Nine Choirs of Angels, as they came to be called, are classified under three heads: Counsellors, Governors, and Messengers:

Group I

The Counsellors include three orders—Seraphim, Cherubim, and Thrones. They are said to stand around the throne of God and to have little or no contact with the mundane affairs of mortals. The three orders of the group:

Seraphim—These are heavenly beings based upon description found in Isaiah 6:2, "And above it stood the Seraphims;

157

each one had six wings; with twain he covered his face, and with twain he covered his feet, and with twain did he fly." The usual color of a seraphim is red, and it bears a scroll upon which is written the words of the Prophet Isaiah, "Holy, Holy, Holy is the Lord of Hosts."

Cherubims are pictured with four wings. Based upon the vision recorded in Ezekiel 10: "They are full of eyes with the likeness of a man under their wings." Their color is sapphire blue and usually they stand upon winged wheels and are shown holding an open book.

Thrones are the angels that bear up the throne of God. They are shown with winged wheels, the color of fire, and full of eyes. Often they sit upon golden thrones or hold towers in their hand.

Group II

The Governors or Rulers. This choir is pictured in early church paintings as clad in long white albs, golden girdles, and green stoles. Upon their right hand are rings of gold. Within their right hand they carry a golden scepter, cross-tipped, and in their left hand the letters I C X C meaning Jesus Christ. They wear crowns and sometimes they are pictured carrying globes. They are shown as possessing bodies resembling those of human beings:

Dominions. These angels are clad as described above and carry a sword, a scepter, a cross, and an orb. They are usually crowned and represent the power of God.

Virtues. These angels are frequently pictured in shining armor, carrying battle axes, swords, and spears. They are possessed of invincible courage and their leader is "Hamel."

Powers. These are the protectors of mankind. They bear flaming swords or batons and often hold chains with which they are supposed to bind Satan. They are led by Raphael.

Group III

Messengers—Third Choir of Angels. This choir is composed of the messengers of God. They are shown as soldiers in full armor, human in body, wearing golden girdles, and holding javelins, spears, swords, or lances. They, likewise, are divided into three classes:

Principalities. These are ministering angels shown as winged human beings and clad in armor. They carry a scepter, a cross, palms, vials, or a lily. They are protectors of rulers and their leader is Chamall.

Archangels. These are winged beings with human bodies, clad in full armor. They are led by St. Michael. He was the protector of the Jewish nation and in Christian times was accepted as the guardian angel of the church. Many churches are dedicated to him.

St. Gabriel. "God is my strength." He is the great Archangel who is believed to stand in the presence of God. He represents the royal dignity of God and is the messenger angel par excellence. He is pictured thousands of times as the messenger of Annunciation, a fact which is entirely Scriptural. He carries a lily and a scepter, sometimes an olive or palm branch. He wears a cape and alb. He is the Angel of the Day of Judgment and when thus shown, bears a trumpet.

ECCLESIASTICAL COLORS

The Christian Church today has five ceremonial colors—white, red, green, violet, and black. White is used during Easter and Christmas, also on circumcision and Epiphany of our Lord. It is the most joyous of all the colors used in the Christian Church. White is the symbol of innocence, purity, virginity, faith, joy, life, and light. In art the Virgin Mary is robed in white at her Assumption.

Red is used on the Exaltation of the Cross and at the feast of Pentecost. It is symbolic of our Lord's Passion and denotes divine love, power, regal dignity, war, and suffering.

Green is used on common Sundays and ordinary weekdays. It signifies hope, plenty, mirth, youth, and prosperity. As the color of living vegetation, green was adopted as a symbol of life. Angels and saints are frequently clad in green, particularly Saint John.

Violet or purple is used on Ash Wednesday and during Lent, Holy Week, and Advent. It is said to symbolize the union of love and pain in repentance, passion, suffering, humility, and truth. Angels wear violet when they call men to repentance or share in the sorrow of our Lord.

Black is the fifth canonical color, but it is only used on Good Friday. It symbolizes death, despair, sorrow, and mourning.

Blue was originally a canonical color but is now rarely used by the church. It is the symbol of Heaven and signifies sincerity, godliness, and piety.

Yellow, when pure, signifies brightness, goodness, faith, and fruitfulness. When of a dingy or dull tone, it symbolizes deceit and jealousy. In medieval art, Judas is usually habited in a dingy yellow garment.

SUGGESTED SOURCES FOR
ADDITIONAL HOLIDAY MATERIAL

CATHOLIC HOLIDAYS

Monks, James. *Great Catholic Festivals*. New York: Henry Shuman Co., 1958.

Weiser, Francis X. *The Christmas Book*, 1952, *The Easter Book*, 1954, *The Holiday Book*, 1956. New York: Harcourt, Brace and Company.

National Catholic Welfare Council, 1312 Massachusetts Ave., Washington, D.C.

JEWISH HOLIDAYS

Coopersmith, H. *The New Jewish Song Book*, 1964, *Hebrew Songster*, 1948. New York: Jewish Educational Committee.

Gilbert, Arthur, and Tarcov, Oscar. *Your Neighbor Celebrates*. New York: Friendly House Publications, 1957.

Lapson, Dvora. *Folk Dances For Jewish Festivals*, 1961, *Jewish Dances the Year Around*, 1957, *Dances of the Jewish People*, 1954. New York: Jewish Educational Committee.

Anti-Defamation League, 315 Lexington Ave., New York, N.Y. *Numerous pamphlets on Jewish Holidays*.

National Conference of Christians and Jews, 43 West 57th street, New York, N.Y.

PROTESTANT HOLIDAYS

Seidenspinner, Clarence. *Great Protestant Festivals*. New York: Henry Shuman Company, 1952